Country Cooking in MENDOCINO

Recipes from
Mendocino County's
renowned caterer
Jeanette Stroh

Enjoy! Debbie Reardan

by Debbie Reardan

This book is dedicated to my mom, Jeanette Stroh, whose passion for cooking was deep within her heart and soul. May the legacy of her cooking and her love for food, family and friends continue on through these wonderful recipes.

ISBN:
0-9788641-0-7
978-0-9788641-0-1

Published by
Deborah Nancy Reardan
Potter Valley, CA 95469

1st Printing Sept. 2006
2nd Printing Dec. 2006

Art and illustrations by Victoria Hand of Victoria Hand Design

Front Cover: A country picnic with a view of Mendocino County, from the oak woodlands to the Pacific Ocean

Back Cover: Photo of Jeanette Stroh by Kent Porter
© *The Press Democrat,* Santa Rosa, CA
Photo of Stroh Ranch by Ken Stroh

WIMMER
COOKBOOKS

A CONSOLIDATED GRAPHICS COMPANY

800.548.2537   wimmerco.com

TABLE OF CONTENTS

INTRODUCTION

*"The recipes in this cookbook are tried and true
from me to you."* ~ Jeanette Stroh, December 2004

This quote from my mom, Jeanette Stroh, sums up what you will find in this cookbook. A catering business truly tests a recipe. From parties of 10 to parties of 500, these recipes were tested and refined, under all sorts of conditions, over the 20 years of Jeanette's Country Cooking. Before she passed away on January 27, 2005, Mom pulled me to her side and asked me to be sure to include her quote somewhere in the cookbook because she wanted everyone to know how passionate she was about her cooking and her recipes.

In 1998 I started helping Mom with Jeanette's Country Cooking. I worked on food preparation and worked many of her evening parties. One day while prepping, I thought it would be handy to have a book of the recipes we used every day. Many of her recipes were tucked in between pages or stuffed into small crocks. I re-typed most of her recipes on the computer and placed them in a binder with plastic covers. A few years later my computer crashed and to my disappointment I found out the backup disk I had made was unreadable. All of that work was gone.

Over the years we stuffed new recipes into the binder and updated the originals. Thank goodness we had that first binder. In 2004, Mom started talking more about retiring from catering. We had already talked about writing a cookbook together and releasing it on the day she retired. In the spring of 2004, we recruited my niece, Shara Madigan, to type the recipes from the binder into the computer. I made a long list of the recipes I needed to have Mom write down, since so many of Mom's recipes were in her head. We didn't know that we were going to lose her to kidney cancer eight months later.

I knew I was going to write my mom's cookbook as a legacy to her, I just didn't know when. Those months after Mom's passing were difficult for me. She was not only my mom, but also my best friend and my business partner. In August, 2005 it suddenly hit me that it was time to start.

iv

Writing the book turned out to be very cathartic. Mom's recipes made her come alive in me again. I felt the happy times I had growing up. I tasted her amazing cooking. Mom and I always talked about how food can make any event better; it makes us feel good and brings people closer together. It happened to me while writing. I was inspired enough to spend hours in the kitchen testing recipes. My husband John, daughter Amanda, dad Ken Stroh, and our friends Marty and Nancy Smith became my main tasters.

Finding all of these recipes was a challenge. I was frustrated that I had a long list of recipes that we didn't have written down on paper. I decided to do more sleuthing. I called her friends, went through every nook and cranny in the catering kitchen, and read through old articles that had been written about Mom. Through those efforts I was able to find or re-create 42 of the 54 recipes on my original list. I even found additional old recipes that I had grown up with that weren't on the list. I was ecstatic every time I found an original recipe. I began feeling more and more confident with this cookbook.

I decided that most of the recipes needed to be tested. Many of them were written for serving 50, 100 or 150 people. Mom was great at working a recipe for 10 people into a recipe for 200; it truly takes a special skill. The original recipe was long gone. My challenge was to shrink portions back down to a 13x9x2-inch baking dish or a small bowl for 10 people. Over the 11 months of writing this cookbook, I tested 188 of the 206 recipes; the other 18 were ones I knew well. My confidence level soared after finishing the testing process. I had proven my mom's quote is definitely true!

Throughout the book you will notice a pig theme. Mom collected pigs over her 20 years of catering. The pig in the cookbook has a personality of her own and even has a name. Penny the pig is the hand-drawn creation of Victoria Hand of Victoria Hand Designs. Penny is holding every page number on her platter and is most active on the divider pages. We still have Mom's extensive pig collection in the houses and in the catering kitchen. From salt and pepper shakers to platters, to the weather vane on top of the kitchen, pigs are everywhere.

I loved writing this book. I can whip together any of the recipes very quickly now, and I'm sure I have the best stocked spice cabinet in all of Mendocino County. I am proud of my mom and the accomplishments she made with her successful catering business. I know these are great recipes from one of the greatest country chefs around.

Enjoy!

Debbie Reardan

vi

FOREWORD

By John and Margarett Parducci

John and Margarett Parducci have lived in Mendocino County for over 88 years and have been married for 69 years. John and his family founded Parducci Wine Cellars in 1932. John is a third generation winemaker and continues to make classic varietal wines at McNab Ridge Winery in Ukiah. Margarett loves gardening and continues to be active in the community with the Held-Poage Memorial Home and Research Library and Grace Hudson Museum.

We remember the first time we met Jeanette at Parducci Wine Cellars after she and Ken first moved to Mendocino County. She was the slickest chick we had ever seen and so beautiful.

We were thrilled when she and Pat Denny started their catering business in 1986; Jeanette and Pat were two of our closest friends. They catered lunches, dinners, and Sunday brunches at Parducci Wine Cellars. We are proud to say we hired them for their first big job in 1987. It was our 50th wedding anniversary for 450 people at the Ukiah fairgrounds. We believed in Jeanette and Pat and knew our day would be special. They did a beautiful job and worked so well together. In all the years they catered, they never ran short of food!

Through the years, Jeanette became our exclusive, personal caterer. We never wanted anyone else to come into our home to cook. We always made sure Jeanette was available before we scheduled our parties. When we entertained by the pool, Ken would barbecue while Jeanette and her staff ran up and down several flights of stairs to reach the kitchen. Everything she made for us was excellent. She even remembered who was at each of our parties and would change the menus so we always had something new to enjoy.

We truly miss Jeanette. She worked so hard on her recipes, and her successful catering business proved that. Since we've tried most of them over the years, we personally know the recipes in this cookbook are excellent.

vii

ACKNOWLEDGMENTS

My family has supported me throughout the writing of this cookbook. My loving husband John, and daughter Amanda gave me the strength and nurturing I needed to have this dream come true. My dad, Ken Stroh, and his enthusiasm encouraged me to keep on my timeline. My sister Kathy and brother-in-law Dick Williams gave me the input I needed to stay on the right path. My Uncle John and Aunt Litty McRoberts helped me relive Mom's childhood years for the biography, and the entire Reardan family gave me moral support.

Testing (and tasting) recipes is one of the most important parts of a cookbook. I had the best tasters around to make sure Mom's recipes were tested to the highest standards. Thanks to the following taste testers for joining me in adding a few pounds: John Reardan, Amanda Reardan, Ken Stroh, Kathy Williams, Dick Williams, nephew Kenny Madigan, Nancy Smith, Marty Smith, Howard K. Howard, the Reardan family, the Miller family, the Westbrook family, and many more family and friends who enjoyed tastes at our dinner parties. I appreciate Kathy and Dick Williams, Nancy and Marty Smith, and Knox and Luke Miller who helped by making some of the recipes themselves, providing me a needed break during the testing process.

Thanks to my niece, Shara Madigan, who did an incredible job of helping me input Mom's recipes into the computer.

Many of Mom's recipes were not written down, and specifics about Jeanette's Country Cooking were hard to come by. Thankfully, I knew I could count on Raul Gonzalez and Gracia Slater to help me remember the ingredients and reconstruct some of Mom's catering recipes. Dennis Denny, Aunt Jean Ingels, and my dad were instrumental in helping me remember the early catering years of Mom and Pat Denny.

I woke up one morning at 2:30 a.m. with a vision of what I wanted on the front of the cookbook. Graphic designer and artist Victoria Hand had the skill to make my vision into reality. From the front to the back, and from Penny the pig to the divider pages, Victoria did it all with creativity and enthusiasm.

Of course I had a long list of Mom's recipes that I had to include but that I couldn't find. I asked Mom's close friends to search their recipe boxes, and I'm grateful to Karen Moon, Norma Dunsing, Carole Stokes, Mary Louise Chase, Susan Westcott Moon, and Kristi Duncan, who found many of the recipes I remembered.

Mom also had many wonderful friends and family who shared their special recipes over the years. Our family is thankful to Pat and Dennis Denny, Karen and John Moon, Norma and Richard Dunsing, Kay and Ralph Whittaker, Joan and Max Schlienger, Gary Venturi, Raul Gonzalez, Grandma Nancy McRoberts, Grandma Adelaide Stroh, Aunt Annie Laurie, Mary Louise and Leroy Chase, Peggy and Howard K. Howard, Dr. Christison, Martha and Charlie Barra, Father Gary, Tom and Linda Wakeman, Gracia and Kenneth Slater, Judy and Larry Thornton, and Maggie and Rich Hearney. Their recipes are noted in the recipe footnotes.

I asked Mom's friends to submit favorite recipes they knew Mom would love. I tested all of their recipes and they are all as special as these friends. My thanks to Carole and Roy Stokes, Susan Westcott Moon, Nancy and Marty Smith, Barbara Hopper, Cathy Anello, Dolores and Larry Hamilton, and Arlene and Don Colombini. Their recipes are noted in the recipe footnotes.

Since the 1970's, Mom and Dad enjoyed membership in their Supper Club. The group of eight couples met monthly for a gathering of food and friends, and my dad continues to be a member of this very close group. I asked each of the members to submit recipes in honor of Mom. Special thanks to Monte and Kay Hill, John and Karen Moon, Pat Nicholson, Conrad and Joezelle Cox, Dennis Denny and Jette Vinding, Bob and Thelma Levy, and Larry and Judy Artman. Their recipes are noted in the recipe footnotes.

Mom always had a wonderful, dedicated staff, both paid and unpaid. Raul Gonzalez was Mom's first paid employee. He started on the ranch in 1988, and when the catering jobs picked up, he split his time between ranch work and catering. He was like a son to Mom, and worked for her for 17 years. In the early

ix

years of Jeanette's Country Cooking she had the following staff: Betty Reid, Maggie McCamish, Marsha Saldin, Dayna Hafen, Jeannie Canevari, Ann Canevari, Gracia Slater, Judy Thornton, Summer Smith, and numerous friends on call. In the last years of Jeanette's Country Cooking she had Arlene Colombini, Cathy Anello, Dolores Hamilton, Natalie Gallups, Raul Gonzalez, and Moy Gonzalez who all stayed on to the end. Our family will always appreciate the hard work of these friends over the 20 years of Jeanette's Country Cooking.

It was important to me to have pictures in the cookbook of the catering business, staff, Stroh Ranch, and family. Thanks to Ken Stroh, John and Karen Moon, Katrina Duncan, and Dick and Kathy Williams for making this a reality.

The final part of writing a cookbook is editing. Initial editors were John Reardan, Nancy Smith, Ken Stroh, and Barbara Hopper. Nancy and John together edited the entire book. Once the thoughts and recipes were written, Rusty Eddy of Rainmaker Marketing polished and revised the text to where it is today, and Arlene Wade made sure every recipe page was consistent and easy to follow.

Finally, I would like to thank the staff at Wimmer Cookbooks for creatively and efficiently combining all of the ingredients needed to form and print my cookbook.

THROUGH THE YEARS

Jeanette Eleanor Stroh
September 21, 1940 — January 27, 2005

By Debbie Reardan, Daughter

Whenever friends or relatives came for a visit, Mom cooked. She loved the kitchen. And visitors or no, Kathy, Dad, and I knew every meal would be great. We were raised on grass fed beef, potatoes, salads, yeast breads, and desserts every night, thanks to Dad's sweet tooth. Mom tried numerous vegetable recipes on us, and the Brussels sprouts were always the hardest to swallow. I almost think she kept trying to get us to eat Brussels sprouts just so she could laugh about it later. Even her cooking reflected her great sense of humor.

Jeanette Eleanor Stroh was born on September 21, 1940 in Kansas City, Missouri and adopted two months later by Lewis (Mac) and Nancy McRoberts. Along with her new parents, her four-year-old brother John greeted her when she arrived at her new home in Burlingame, California.

Jeanette had a Norman Rockwell childhood: family trips to Montana, camping at Richardson's Grove, Brownies, Girl Scouts (Troop 44) and Methodist services on Sunday. Jeanette learned clarinet, French horn and piano, and generally did everything at a speed faster than most; everyone called her "Jet".

Her love of cooking started as a passion for blending, when at three years old she mixed brother John's prized butterfly collection into a jar of peanut butter to "make it better." Her mother influenced her early love of cooking, later enforced by her high school home economics teacher, and her mother-in-law Adelaide Stroh.

Mom was a natural born athlete with the trophies to prove it. At eight she joined the Peninsula Tennis Club. At 10 and 16 she won the state championship. She played against Billie Jean King several times and won twice. Uncle John played her several times but doesn't remember scoring any points. She always asked him if he wanted her to "play soft." He always answered, "No, play me regular."

xi

Her decision to go to Willamette University to study home economics for a year probably prevented her from going professional.

Mom met my dad, Ken Stroh, at Burlingame High when she was 14. She knew immediately she had met the man she would marry. She made good on her promise five years later when they were married on May 21, 1960. Their honeymoon at Clearlake was interrupted by Dad's brother and sister and a group of friends; Mom promptly went to work and cooked for the entire crowd.

Mom and Dad lived in San Mateo and Burlingame while Dad served at Moffett Field Naval Air Station. My sister, Kathy, was born May 19, 1961. I was born January 3, 1966. The family moved around California's north coast for a few years, finally settling on the 3400-acre Potter Valley ranch in 1967.

Life on a ranch is a challenge even without children. Mom and Dad had to evict the skunks and rattlesnakes in the 900-square foot cabin prior to moving in, but they made it a great family home. Aside from us kids, Mom and Dad raised 160 head of beef cattle and grew sweet corn, vegetables, and hay. The corn and vegetables supplied a summer produce stand that became a great family institution.

When Mom wasn't farming or cooking she had her hobbies. There was the Deerwood Tennis Club, the yarn shop, and her collection of glass insulators. Mom canned every summer, and we filled the cabinets with dilled pickles, tomatoes, tomato sauce, peaches, pears, apricot jam, peach jam, and the family favorite — wild blackberry jam.

We kids grew vegetables to enter in the annual County Fair competition while Mom produced a variety of baked goods to compete. She enjoyed telling the story of missing first place one year because her pie crust was "too flaky."

Mom actively supported the Grange and the PTA. She and Dad went to every local basketball, volleyball and baseball game. She was a 4-H leader for cooking and knitting, and she coached Kathy's volleyball team. She was an animal lover and nursed injured wildlife, including green herons, an owl named Mr. Puff, a

XII

pigeon named Pidgie, and a turkey named Walter. I think people knew Mom's reputation and consciously dropped animals off near our property.

Besides food and cooking, Mom was passionate about knitting. She was still knitting two months before she passed away. She made beautiful sweaters and blankets, and she even made us bathing suits when we were kids, though the bottoms ended up at our ankles. Mom started Country Crafts of Potter Valley in 1982 to sell sweaters, afghans, and ornaments to the neighbors, and she dabbled in making pies and cookies for local stores and restaurants.

The Classic Country Cook

Inevitably, Mom's passions blended together. She started catering part time while continuing to make the pies, sugar cookies, and craft items. In 1986 she started Country Cooking and Crafts with her good friend Pat Denny. The business prospered, and the County noticed. So when they cited her for catering out of her own kitchen she decided to build a commercial catering kitchen on the ranch. Dad and my Uncle Lyle Ingels built the 700-square foot kitchen, and the County approved it in 1987.

Inside, windows faced north, east and south. Stainless counters, a huge Wolf stove, a new freezer and refrigerator, shelves, a large pantry, and a new convection oven for making pies and cookies, beckoned. Mom filled the shelves with plates, platters, utensils, chafing dishes, transporters, pots, and pans. She decorated it all with a pig theme and called it her second home.

The new kitchen fueled the growth of the business. They catered John and Margaret Parducci's 50th wedding anniversary and numerous wine and food events at Parducci Wine Cellars. At one event the winery invited food editors from *Better Homes and Gardens, Bon Appétit, Country Living, Good Food Magazine* and *Ladies Home Journal*. Mom and Pat wowed the guests with Sausage "Stroh"del, Fruit Dip with fresh fruit, Dried Fruit Medley Cake, Wild Rice Pudding, and Country Sunrise for dessert *(see index for recipes)*.

XIII

PJ's Gourmet

Mendocino County loves a good barbecue, and Country Cooking and Crafts flourished. Mom and Pat developed a marinade to complement the tri-tip they barbecued, which became Stroh Ranch Original Marinade. They started PJ's Gourmet (Pat and Jeanette) in January of 1992 to sell the marinade locally. Pat spearheaded PJ's Gourmet, while Mom continued catering.

Sadly, Pat passed away in 1997. Her husband graciously gifted her partnership in PJ's Gourmet to me to keep the business in our family. What a wonderful experience to suddenly have my mom as my business partner! We had a ball attending food and wine events from Mendocino County to San Francisco. Attendees lined up 20 deep for tastes of our marinated tri-tip hot off the grill. In 2000, Mom and I started making Stroh Ranch Wild Blackberry Jam and later released Stroh Ranch Razzleberry Jam and Stroh Ranch Raspberry Jam. In 2001 we released Stroh Ranch Smoky Jalapeno Honey Sauces, dipping sauces from the catering business that we used with gourmet sausages.

Jeanette's Country Cooking

In 1992 Mom became the sole proprietor of her business, Jeanette's Country Cooking of Potter Valley. The cattle had been sold and the family was farming and catering full time. Kathy and I helped whenever we were home. I was a college graduate living in Woodland, California. It was understood that when we came home for the weekend there was catering going on. If we wanted to see Mom, we walked to the catering kitchen anytime between 6 a.m. and 3 p.m. If we wanted to see Dad, we strolled to the barbecue where he'd be grilling tri-tip, ribs, or chicken.

Mom continued making baked goods for local stores. She made potato and macaroni salads for local delis and made lasagnas for a local pizzeria. Mom's pie baking record was 88 in one day, all different types. She began having more events at the ranch, including car rallies, Chamber of Commerce mixers, weddings, reunions, and tacky parties. Following a local forest fire she fed

exhausted firefighters, and she hosted a film crew on a break from a Ford truck commercial. She even had the opportunity to cook for Chuck Yeager and astronaut Charles Bolden.

Mom's greatest fear was running out of food at an event. She vowed never to let that happen and made sure she always had plenty of food. She wanted to be ready when 20 extra people dropped in. And she always planned for enough extra to feed her staff and their families, the DJ, and the bartender.

Mom considered herself a country cook. She said Country was her style and that it was simpler and tasted better. Of course "Country" meant meat and potatoes, local produce, and big portions. People wanted fresh produce and wholesome meats and chicken, not a lot of fancy gourmet, saucy-type food. Some of her customers' favorite requests were Ken and Jeanette's BBQ Tri-Tip with Stroh Ranch Original Marinade, Stuffed Mushrooms, Garlic Dip, Caesar Salad, Potato Salad, Macaroni Salad, seasonal fresh fruit salad and homemade desserts (see index for recipes). A typical dinner would be half a dozen hot and cold hors d'oeuvres, an entrée, a side dish, two kinds of salads, garlic bread or dinner rolls made by our local bakeries, and homemade dessert — all for a very reasonable price.

Away from the kitchen you could find Mom reading either a bestseller or a cookbook. Her cookbook collection numbered over 3000. Cookbooks are still spread everywhere on the ranch. All she ever wanted for Christmas, Mother's Day or her birthday was a cookbook. It was a challenge to find one she didn't have, since she bought them as souvenirs everywhere she traveled. She knew right away if a recipe could be adapted for catering or not, and she altered recipes to suit her taste. Her favorite cookbooks were Junior League collections from all around the country. For the basics she relied on Betty Crocker.

Mom was very humble about her successful catering business. In a local newspaper article, she said, "I simply love what I'm doing. I always have. I cook the way I always have. At heart, I'm a meat and potatoes girl. I don't ever want someone to walk away from my table hungry." She relished the

compliments she received after an event, but never expected them. I'm still amazed at how she orchestrated everything from menu planning and ordering food to prepping and organizing staff — all without a computer. Her invoices were hand-written, and ordering was done over the phone.

When Mom was diagnosed with kidney cancer in September 2004, she decided it was best to stick with our family doctors in the Sacramento area. She lived with my sister, Kathy, and her husband Dick for the four months she underwent treatment. Dad stayed with Mom as much as possible. I stayed on the ranch and kept Jeanette's Country Cooking going. We had thousands to feed over the holidays, and we were determined to keep our commitments. Of course I had to be in close contact with Mom for help with ordering and recipe development.

We all hoped Mom would beat cancer. We planned to get through chemotherapy and have her back in the kitchen in the fall. She never had that opportunity. Mom passed away on January 27, 2005.

Jeanette's Country Cooking's last catering job was in 2005 for the St. Mary's Church fundraiser. Four hundred fifty people attended, many who knew Mom and all of whom gave us a standing ovation. They honored my mom. We loved my mom and her cooking, and we knew, at that minute, we were definitely not alone; she had truly touched our community. Jeanette's Country Cooking closed on February 20, 2005.

Mom was fortunate to always have a dedicated staff. This staff tribute to my mom, written by Cathy Anello, Dolores Hamilton, and Arlene Colombini, and read at her memorial service, sums up the feelings of those who worked for Mom over the years:

It's no secret that Jeanette's Country Cooking was the best catering company in town, and that we had the best time working for her. For most of us it was our second job of the week, which is, I think now a great accolade to how we felt about our jobs and about Jeanette. Now, most people get tired of their jobs after a while but when you were working for Jeanette on a Friday night, even after a long day at another job, something magical would happen. No matter how tired you were, we would kick into party gear and a second wind would hit you. Now of course it's not often you arrive to work and get paid before you start, get handed a lottery ticket with the promise of a new car if she won and then after attending some of the best parties in Ukiah, having enough food to go home and feed your family every week. There was always a sense of pride when working for Jeanette. Her desire to give her customers excellence, and her high standards extended to her staff. Our performance on the job was an absolute extension of her. We were the best, because she was the best.

Mom's kitchen still looks just like it did when she was here. Her cookbooks and pigs are everywhere. I love it. The kitchen is still a certified commercial food facility, and I will continue operating PJ's Gourmet Specialty Foods (www.pjsgourmet.com), making the marinade and jams in the kitchen. It is not the same without Mom, but I feel her every time I walk in.

We always felt the love Mom had for us. She always supported us, and we miss her greatly. We hope the legacy of her country cooking continues through her recipes in this cookbook.

XVII

Jeanette's Country Cooking

Jeanette's commercial catering kitchen on Stroh Ranch

Jeanette barbecuing tri-tips on Stroh Ranch in 1996 with Stroh Ranch Original Marinade

Pat Denny and Jeanette Stroh in 1987

Enjoying a wine break during a food and wine event in 1993 with friends, Karen and John Moon, daughter Debbie Reardan, husband Ken Stroh and Jeanette

Jeanette's Country Cooking from left to right: Arlene Colombini, Summer Smith, Mary Gustafson, Gracia Slater, Maggie McCamish, and Betsy Sweaza

Catering at Fetzer Valley Oaks in 1987 with Dozie McFadden, Karen Moon, Kathy Dimier, Jeanette, and Tom McFadden

Raul Gonzalez at one of his first catering jobs with John Moon

Jeanette's favorite cat, Bootsie, with his stuffed twin

Stroh Ranch

A southwest view of Stroh Ranch in Potter Valley

The catering kitchen and shop area with the cornfield in the background

Farming on Stroh Ranch

Bales of hay in one of the pastures

Jeanette and Family

Thanksgiving 2004 with son-in-law John Reardan, daughter Kathy Williams, Jeanette, Ken, and daughter Debbie Reardan

The welcome sign at the kitchen's front door

Jeanette and Ken enjoying a DC-3 airplane ride in 2003

Newlyweds Dick and Kathy Williams in 2004

Grandchildren Amanda Reardan, and Kenny and Shara Madigan

John, Debbie & Amanda Reardan in Tahoe in 2004

Jeanette's Mom, Nancy McRoberts, with young Shara and Kenny

Jeanette's father, Lewis "Mac" McRoberts

Kathy with her children, Kenny and Shara

Jeanette's in-laws, Gerry and Adelaide Stroh

The kitchen's weather vane

Jeanette's sister-in-law Litty and brother, John McRoberts, with Amanda Reardan

The Stroh Girls: Debbie, Kathy and Jeanette

Jeanette taking granddaughter Amanda for a walk on Stroh Ranch in 2003

Debbie with Amanda on Mother's Day 2003

A foggy view of Potter Valley from Ken and Jeanette's deck

Appetizers

CONTENTS

APPETIZERS

Mushroom Tarts

Yields: 48 tarts

Dough

2½ cups all-purpose flour
¼ teaspoon salt
⅔ cup butter
⅓ cup sour cream
1 egg, slightly beaten

Mushroom Mixture

¼ cup butter
½ pound finely chopped fresh mushrooms
3 tablespoons minced green onions
¼ cup all-purpose flour
½ teaspoon salt
1 cup whipping cream

Preheat oven to 400 degrees. In a small bowl, mix together flour and salt. Cut in butter until mixture resembles the size of peas. Stir in sour cream and egg with a fork. Press dough into a ball. Using a tart pan, drop dough by rounded teaspoonfuls into each hole. Press dough onto bottom and up sides of tart pan to make a shell. Bake 12-15 minutes or until golden browned. For the mushroom mixture, melt butter in a sauté pan. Sauté mushrooms and onions 5 minutes. Remove from heat and stir in flour and salt. Gradually add whipping cream and stir until smooth. Spoon mushroom mixture into shells. Place shells on a baking sheet. Bake for 12 minutes. Serve warm or at room temperature on a platter.

Pat Denny and Mom served this recipe many times when they first started the catering business. These tarts are labor intensive but are well worth the time. They taste great and look beautiful on a glass platter.

East-West Sausage

Yields: Filling for 48 cream puffs

1 **pound sausage, cooked, drained, cooled and crumbled**

1 **can (5 ounces) dry chow mein noodles, crushed into small pieces**

1 **cup grated Cheddar cheese**

1 **cup grated mozzarella cheese**

½ **cup mayonnaise**

½ **cup chopped green onions**

Preheat oven to 350 degrees. Combine sausage, noodles, Cheddar cheese, mozzarella cheese, mayonnaise, and onions in a large mixing bowl. Fill sliced cream puffs *(see Cream Puff recipe, page 27)* by teaspoonfuls. Place 1-inch apart on baking sheet. Bake for 10 minutes.

This is an old and true recipe that I was so happy to find. We could not wait for guests to come for dinner so that Mom would make these! I luckily found it printed with an old article our local paper had written about Mom.

APPETIZERS

Antipasto with Tuna

Serves: 12

1 cup water
1 cup white vinegar
1 cup sliced celery
1 cup sliced onions
1 cup sliced carrots
1 can (3.8 ounces) sliced olives
1 jar (12 ounces) sweet whole pickles, chopped
1 bottle (14 ounces) ketchup
¾ cup canola oil
1 can (12 ounces) albacore tuna, drained
Water crackers

Boil water and vinegar in a saucepan. Add celery, onions, and carrots. Return to boil and cook, covered, 15 minutes or until slightly tender. Drain vegetables and cool. Combine vegetables, olives, pickles, ketchup, and oil in a bowl. Add albacore and toss lightly. Refrigerate at least four hours. Serve with water crackers.

The literal meaning of antipasto is "before the meal." This Italian term refers to hot or cold appetizers. There was a note on the recipe that stated this is very good. I'm not sure where the recipe came from, but again I wanted to place recipes in here on which Mom had written "good." This is a unique recipe and one that all of my tasters enjoyed. It is very sweet and tastes great with the tuna.

Cornbread Biscuits with a Red Pepper Spread and Prosciutto

Yields: 24 Biscuits

Biscuit Dough

1 ½ cups all-purpose flour
½ cup yellow cornmeal
1 tablespoon sugar
1 teaspoon salt
1 teaspoon chili powder
1 tablespoon baking powder
½ cup vegetable shortening
1 jalapeño pepper, seeded and minced
¾ cup milk

Red Pepper Spread

¼ jar (15 ounces) roasted red bell peppers
½ cup chopped green onions
¼ cup mayonnaise or more
Salt and pepper to taste
5 ounces sliced prosciutto

Preheat oven to 350 degrees. Combine flour, cornmeal, sugar, salt, chili powder, and baking powder. Cut in shortening until mixture is crumbly. Add jalapeños and milk until a ball forms. The dough will be slightly sticky. Turn dough onto a floured board and knead 2 times while adding enough flour so it will be easy to roll. Roll out dough into a 10-inch diameter circle. Cut dough with a 1 ½-inch biscuit cutter. Roll loose dough pieces back into a circle. Bake 12 minutes or until golden browned. Blend bell peppers, green onions, and mayonnaise in a food processor until creamy. Add salt and pepper. Slice biscuits in half and spread the mixture on one side. Top with a slice of prosciutto and place other half of biscuit on top.

Mom added her personal touch to this recipe she received at a Napa College cooking class. She enjoyed taking appetizer classes. The biscuits are great alone and, of course, they taste their best when you add the spread and prosciutto.

Mushroom Rolls   Serves: 20

1 pound mushrooms, finely chopped

½ cup butter

6 tablespoons all-purpose flour

1½ teaspoons salt

2 cups half-and-half

2 teaspoons lemon juice

1 teaspoon onion salt

1½ loaves sliced white sandwich bread, crust removed

4 tablespoons butter, melted

Preheat oven to 400 degrees. Sauté mushrooms in butter for 5 minutes. Add flour and salt and mix well. Stir in half-and-half and cook until thickened. Add lemon juice and onion salt and let cool. Roll each bread slice very thin with a rolling pin. Spread mushroom mixture on each slice and roll up. Place seam side down on a baking sheet. Place baking sheet in the freezer for 10 minutes. Slice rolls into three pieces leaving seam side down on the baking sheet. Brush with butter. Bake 15-20 minutes or until golden browned and crunchy.

Our family friends, Joan and Max Schlienger, shared this recipe with Mom several years ago. Max was Mom's "President" of Jeanette's Country Cooking, a self-appointed position! He loved her cooking and wanted to be as close as possible to the catering business. The rolls have a delightfully delicate flavor. Save any sauce you may have left over for your eggs the next morning! Joan makes the rolls ahead and freezes them without the melted butter. When she needs them, she thaws and cuts them into thirds and then brushes them with the butter. She suggests serving them with your favorite aïoli sauce.

Cheese Twists

1   **cup butter, softened**
1   **package (8 ounces) cream cheese, softened**
½   **teaspoon salt**
2   **cups all-purpose flour**
1   **cup grated Parmesan cheese**
1   **egg yolk, beaten**
2   **teaspoons milk**

Preheat oven to 350 degrees. Cream butter, cream cheese, salt, and flour in a bowl. Place Parmesan cheese in a measuring cup. In another bowl, whisk together egg yolk and milk. Set aside. Divide dough in half. Roll each half into a rectangle ¼-inch thick on a large lightly floured cutting board. Sprinkle one-third cheese evenly over the two rectangles.

Using a rolling pin, lightly press the cheese into the dough. Fold each rectangle into thirds and roll out again into 2 rectangles. Sprinkle both with one-third cheese, press with rolling pin and fold into thirds. Roll each dough half into an 8x5-inch rectangle. Make sure the folds have rolled together completely so there are no layers inside the dough. Brush each rectangle with egg wash. Sprinkle with remaining cheese. Cut into strips about three-fourths inches wide. Twist strips into spirals and place on an ungreased baking sheet. Bake for 15-20 minutes. Serve warm.

I love the sharp flavor of the Parmesan cheese in these twists. I think they taste their best when served warm with a light white wine!

8

Ham Stacks

Serves: 6

1   package (8 ounces) cream cheese, softened

2   teaspoons dehydrated minced onions

¼   teaspoon garlic salt

Dash of pepper

1   package (8 ounces) sliced cooked ham (8 slices)

1   teaspoon dried parsley

Blend cream cheese, onions, garlic salt, and pepper until creamy. Remove the ham from the package and pat dry each piece with a paper towel. Place ham in two piles of four slices to make two ham stacks. Divide cream cheese in half for each ham stack. Place one slice of ham on a cutting board. Spread an even layer of the cream cheese mixture over it and place another ham slice on top. Repeat with a layer of cream cheese mixture and ham slice and place the fourth slice of ham on top. Repeat the layers with the second pile of ham and cream cheese mixture. Sprinkle parsley evenly over the top two pieces of ham. Wrap the two stacks separately with plastic wrap and refrigerate 1 hour. Cut each stack into 16 pieces. Separate the pieces and serve on a chilled platter.

My sister, Kathy Williams, thankfully remembered how to make this favorite appetizer from our childhood. Mom always used packaged ham from our local stores. Kathy suggests not using a sweet or flavored ham. Sometimes Mom would cut the stacks into squares or triangles. Both ways look pretty on a platter.

Artichoke Heart Soufflé

Serves: 10

2 jars (6 ounces each) marinated artichoke hearts

1 medium yellow onion, chopped

3 garlic cloves, minced

4 eggs, beaten

½ cup unseasoned bread crumbs

2 tablespoons minced fresh parsley

⅛ teaspoon hot pepper sauce

1 package (8 ounces) shredded Cheddar cheese

Preheat oven to 350 degrees. Drain liquid from one jar of artichoke hearts into a bowl. Drain and discard liquid from second jar. Chop all artichokes into small pieces. Add onions and garlic to liquid and set aside for 5 minutes. Combine chopped artichoke hearts, eggs, bread crumbs, parsley, hot pepper sauce, and Cheddar cheese in a large bowl. Add onion and garlic mixture and mix well. Spread mixture evenly into a greased 13x9x2-inch baking dish. Bake for 30 minutes. Let stand 20 minutes. Cut into bite size squares. Serve at room temperature.

Mom's close friend, Gary Venturi, shared this recipe with her. Gary, who is an amazing cook, was the innkeeper for La Chaumiere Bed and Breakfast in Calistoga for over 12 years. Mom and Dad would go there for some rest and relaxation and enjoyed every meal that Gary created. This recipe was one that Gary served to his guests when they arrived. He also served it as a main course for breakfast.

10

Pesto Cheesecake

Serves: 18

1 tablespoon butter, softened

1/4 cup fine dry bread crumbs

2 tablespoons freshly grated Parmesan cheese

2 packages (8 ounces each) cream cheese, softened

1/2 cup freshly grated Parmesan cheese

1/4 teaspoon garlic salt

1/2 teaspoon hot pepper sauce

3 large eggs

1/2 cup pesto sauce

1 package (8 ounces) cream cheese, softened

Fresh basil sprigs for garnish

1/4 cup pine nuts for garnish

Assorted crackers

Preheat oven to 325 degrees. Rub butter over bottom and sides of a 9-inch springform pan. Combine bread crumbs and Parmesan cheese. Coat the pan with crumb mixture. Using an electric mixer, beat cream cheese, Parmesan cheese, garlic salt, and hot pepper sauce until light and fluffy. Add eggs one at a time, beating well after each addition. Transfer half cream cheese mixture to medium bowl. Stir pesto into remaining half. Spoon pesto mixture into prepared pan smoothing out top. Carefully spread remaining cream cheese mixture on top smoothing to edges. Bake 45 minutes or until center is set. Transfer to rack and cool completely. Cover tightly with plastic wrap and refrigerate overnight. Run small sharp knife around sides to loosen cheesecake, if necessary. Release pan sides from cheesecake. Transfer cheesecake to platter. Spread plain cream cheese evenly over top and garnish with basil sprigs and pine nuts. Surround with crackers and serve.

This was one of my mom's favorite recipes, one that she was very proud of. Sometimes we would ice the entire cake with cream cheese. This takes more cream cheese than the recipe states, but makes it look very pretty all white.

11

Garlic Dip

Serves: 10

1 cup chopped artichoke hearts

2 packages (8 ounces each) shredded Monterey Jack cheese

½ cup grated Parmesan cheese

10 garlic cloves, chopped

¼ cup mayonnaise to bind

2 teaspoons dried parsley

Assorted crackers

Preheat oven to 350 degrees. Combine artichoke hearts, Jack cheese, Parmesan cheese, garlic, and mayonnaise in a bowl. Spread mixture evenly in a quiche pan. Sprinkle parsley on top. Bake 30 minutes or until heated through and lightly golden browned. Absorb oil on top with a paper towel. Serve warm with crackers.

Here is the recipe you have all been waiting for! So many people have wanted this recipe since the beginning of Jeanette's Country Cooking. This is Mom's signature dish and one that is always a crowd pleaser. It is great the next morning served with eggs.

12

APPETIZERS

Beau Monde Dip

Serves: 15

1 package (8 ounces) cream cheese, softened

1 cup mayonnaise

1 cup sour cream

2 tablespoons dried minced onions

2 teaspoons Beau Monde seasoning

1 cup water chestnuts, finely chopped

1 package (10 ounces) frozen chopped spinach, thawed and squeezed dry

Assorted crackers or French bread pieces

Blend cream cheese, mayonnaise, sour cream, onions, and beau monde seasoning in a food processor until smooth. Add water chestnuts and spinach. Pulse on and off quickly and leave mixture chunky. Serve in a bowl with your favorite crackers or pieces of French bread.

This dip is similar to a leek soup dip, but more flavorful. The beau monde seasoning adds to this very popular dip.

13

Olive Cheese Ball

Serves: 10

- **1 package (8 ounces) cream cheese, softened**
- **8 ounces crumbled blue cheese, softened**
- **¼ cup butter, softened**
- **1 cup chopped black olives**
- **1 tablespoon chopped fresh parsley**
- **4 green onions, chopped**
- **¾ cup walnuts, chopped**
- **Assorted crackers**

Blend cream cheese, blue cheese, butter, olives, parsley, and green onions. Refrigerate about two hours. When chilled, roll cheese mixture into a ball. Place walnuts in a bowl and roll ball in walnuts. Serve chilled on a platter with crackers. This recipe can be made a day ahead.

Our family loves blue cheese so this recipe was a big hit! It tastes best if you can make it a day ahead to enhance the flavors.

14

Curry Crab Mousse

Serves: 10

1 can (10¾ ounces) cream of mushroom soup

1 package (8 ounces) cream cheese

2 tablespoons unflavored gelatin

¼ cup warm water

½ teaspoon salt

2 tablespoons lemon juice

½ teaspoon curry powder

8 ounces cooked crabmeat, minced

½ cup chopped green onions

½ cup chopped celery

1 cup mayonnaise

Assorted crackers

Heat soup and cream cheese in a saucepan until melted and thoroughly combined. Dissolve gelatin in water. Add to soup and mix thoroughly. Pour cream cheese mixture into a bowl. Add salt, juice, curry, crabmeat, green onions, celery, and mayonnaise. Pour mixture into a large mold lined with plastic wrap. Refrigerate until chilled. Invert mousse onto your favorite platter. Serve with crackers.

I love curry, so this became a favorite for me. This was a newer recipe that Mom used a few times in the catering business. She loved crab, so you will find several crab appetizers in this book. We could get fresh Dungeness crab from our wonderful fleet of fishermen on the Mendocino coast in season over the winter months.

15

Pecan and Cheese Spread

Serves: 8

1 **package (8 ounces) shredded Cheddar cheese**

4 **ounces cream cheese, softened**

2 **tablespoons mayonnaise**

1/8 **teaspoon hot pepper sauce**

1/8 **teaspoon Worcestershire sauce**

4 **slices bacon, cooked crisp and crumbled**

3 **green onions, sliced**

1/2 **cup chopped pecans**

Assorted crackers

Blend Cheddar cheese, cream cheese, mayonnaise, hot pepper sauce, and Worcestershire sauce in a food processor. Pour into a bowl. Stir in bacon and green onions. Pour pecans into a shallow bowl. Shape cheese mixture into a ball and roll in the pecans. Serve with your favorite crackers.

This is a very mild tasting cheese ball and very tasty with the bacon and pecans. Just add more hot pepper sauce to give it a spicier flavor.

16

Avocado Pâté with Parsley and Pistachios   Serves: 10

4	ripe avocados, pitted and peeled
2	packages (8 ounces each) cream cheese, softened
2	tablespoons minced shallots
1	tablespoon fresh lemon juice
2	teaspoons minced garlic
1	teaspoon chili powder
½	teaspoon salt
¼	cup chopped fresh parsley
2	tablespoons chopped unsalted pistachios
4	butter lettuce leaves
½	cup pitted black olives
10	ripe cherry tomatoes
Tortilla chips	

Line a 9x5-inch glass loaf pan or ceramic dish with 3 layers of wax paper, extending over long sides only. Brush top sheet of paper generously with oil. Purée avocados and cream cheese in food processor. Add shallots, lemon juice, garlic, chili powder, and salt. Blend 30 seconds. Pour mixture into prepared pan, smoothing out top. Cover the surface with plastic wrap. Refrigerate at least 6 hours. Remove plastic from pâté. Turn mold over onto a rectangular platter. Remove wax paper. Combine parsley and pistachios. Sprinkle over pâté. Arrange lettuce decoratively at corners of platter. Garnish with olives and tomatoes. Surround with tortilla chips.

What a wonderful, creamy appetizer this is. It makes you want to spread it everywhere you spread butter! My husband and I spread it on our hamburgers the night we tested it and then had it again with chips the next day. If you want it spicier, you can add more shallots or a shot of hot pepper sauce.

Vegetarian Lavosh

Serves: 10

4	packages (3 ounces each) cream cheese, softened
¾	teaspoon seasoned salt
5	(10-inch) tortilla wraps, red and/or green
1	small bunch spinach leaves
8	ounces thinly sliced Monterey Jack cheese
8	ounces thinly sliced Cheddar cheese
1	small red onion, thinly sliced
1	sweet red pepper, seeded, thinly sliced
1	yellow pepper, seeded, thinly sliced
1	bell pepper, seeded, thinly sliced
2	carrots, peeled and grated
1	package (4 ounces) alfalfa sprouts

Blend cream cheese and seasoned salt in a small bowl. Spread cream cheese mixture evenly on each tortilla. Arrange a thin layer of spinach leaves over cream cheese. Layer both cheeses over spinach. Top each tortilla with a thin layer of onions, peppers, carrots, and sprouts. Roll up tortilla and place seam side down on a cutting board. Cut each into 8 slices. Arrange slices flat on a platter and refrigerate. Serve cold.

Mom always called these delicious pinwheel appetizers "lavosh" because she often used the Armenian cracker bread to make them. Lavosh is traditionally made from round, thin, crisp breads. In the last few years of catering, she began using the large colorful tortilla wraps that are listed in the ingredient list. They come in various colors, mostly red, green, and tan. Another variation is to make these appetizers with only meat. She used sliced cheese, ham, and turkey with the cream cheese and salt.

18

Raul's Red Salsa

Serves: 10

1 lime, juiced
1 medium yellow onion, chopped
20 Roma tomatoes, diced
1 bunch cilantro, leaves only and chopped
3 Serrano peppers, finely chopped
2 garlic cloves, chopped
1 bell pepper, chopped
1 ½ teaspoons salt
Tortilla chips

Mix lime juice and onions in a bowl and set aside for 10 minutes. In a large bowl, combine tomatoes, cilantro, Serrano peppers, garlic, peppers, and salt. Stir in onions. Refrigerate until chilled. Before serving, stir well and add more salt if needed. Serve with tortilla chips.

Raul Gonzalez is like a brother to me. He came to work on our ranch in 1988 and became Mom's right hand man in the catering business. Mom depended on Raul for the huge amount of prep needed before her catering jobs. He worked for Mom and Dad for 17 years and continues to live on the ranch with his family. He is an amazing cook and prepared all the Mexican dishes for the catering business from scratch. This salsa recipe and all of his family recipes have made him famous in Mendocino County for his authentic Mexican food.

19

Raul's Guacamole

Serves: 10

1 lime, juiced
1 medium yellow onion, chopped
8 avocados, peeled and seeded
1 bunch cilantro, leaves only and chopped
3 jalapeño peppers, seeded and finely chopped
1 pound Roma tomatoes, diced
Salt to taste
Tortilla chips

Mix lime juice and onions in a bowl and set aside for 10 minutes. Place avocados in a large bowl and drag a sharp knife through avocados to cut into small pieces. Stir in cilantro, jalapeños, tomatoes, and onions. Add salt. Transfer to a smaller bowl. Refrigerate until chilled. Serve with tortilla chips.

It was always a treat when Raul made his guacamole. He and his wonderful nephew, Moy Gonzalez, would be up to their eyeballs in avocados making guacamole for several hundred people. These two never complained. They were always smiling and happy. Raul's two unique tricks in this recipe are to mix the lime juice with the onions to cut the sharpness of the onion and using a knife instead of mashing the avocado so it has some chunks in it.

20

APPETIZERS

Raul's Green Tomatillo Salsa

Serves: 10

2   **pounds green tomatillos, peeled and stemmed**

4   **garlic cloves, chopped**

2   **jalapeño peppers, seeded and chopped**

1/2 **bunch cilantro, leaves only and chopped**

1/2 **red onion, minced**

1/2 **teaspoon salt**

Tortilla chips

Cook tomatillos, garlic, and jalapeños in boiling water for 15 minutes. Drain mixture and place in a food processor. Process mixture just until minced. Pour into a bowl. Add cilantro, red onions, and salt. Serve at room temperature with tortilla chips.

Here is another Raul Gonzalez signature recipe! You will love the tangy flavor of this recipe. Tomatillos can be found in specialty produce stores most of the year. Choose ones that are firm with dry, tight fitting husks. They can be stored in the refrigerator in a paper bag for up to a month.

21

Raul's Spicy Tomatillo Salsa

Serves: 10

2 **pounds green tomatillos, peeled and stemmed**

3 **Roma tomatoes**

3-5 **arbol red dried peppers, seeded and stemmed**

6 **garlic cloves**

1 **bunch cilantro, leaves only**

1½ **teaspoons salt**

Tortilla chips

Place tomatillos and tomatoes in boiling water. Reduce heat and simmer 5 minutes. Drain. Combine tomatillos, tomatoes, peppers, garlic, and cilantro in a food processor. Process just until minced. Pour into a bowl and stir in salt. Refrigerate until chilled. Serve with tortilla chips.

"Yum! Yum!" is what Mom wrote on this recipe from Raul Gonzalez. I love the spice of the arbol pepper. For added flavor, Mom suggested charring the dried peppers directly on a stove burner. This recipe is a little spicier than Raul's Green Tomatillo Salsa. Both are excellent recipes. Just add more dried peppers to this recipe to give it more heat.

APPETIZERS

Raul's Mango Salsa

Serves: 10

1   **lime, juiced**
½   **red onion, chopped**
3   **mangos, peeled, seeded and chopped**
1   **papaya, peeled, seeded and chopped**
1   **small pineapple, peeled, cored and chopped**
1   **bunch cilantro, leaves only and chopped**
3   **serrano peppers, seeded and finely chopped**
¼   **cup sugar**
Tortilla chips

Mix lime juice and onions in a small bowl. Set aside. Combine mangos, papaya, pineapple, cilantro, peppers, and sugar in a large bowl. Add onions and mix well. Refrigerate until chilled. Serve with salty tortilla chips.

This is a beautiful and flavorful salsa that will always be a hit at parties. Raul made this for Mom for Hawaiian theme parties. He told me that he also enjoys serving it over a green salad. We think it would be great over grilled swordfish or halibut. For a spicier salsa, just add more chopped serrano peppers.

Hot Cheese Spread

Serves: 10

1 **package (3 ounces) cream cheese, softened**
1 **cup mayonnaise**
1½ **teaspoons grated yellow onion**
⅔ **cup grated Parmesan cheese**
⅛ **teaspoon cayenne pepper**
5 **whole English muffins, cut in half and toasted**

Blend cream cheese, mayonnaise, onions, Parmesan cheese, and cayenne until well combined. Cut each toasted English muffin into 8 pieces making 40 wedges. Spread cheese mixture on each wedge and place on a baking sheet. Broil until browned. Serve hot on a platter.

I love this recipe. I tested it on English muffins and it turned out great. The recipe also calls for slicing a baguette loaf into thin slices and baking at 300 degrees to harden the bread, then spreading the cheese on top and broiling. I know you will enjoy it either way!

24

Turkey Meatballs Glazed with Stroh Ranch Smoky Jalapeño Honey Sauce

Yields: 30 meatballs

1	small yellow onion, chopped
¼	cup butter
2½	pounds lean ground turkey
1	package (7½ ounces) dry seasoned stuffing mix, crushed
1	teaspoon salt
1	teaspoon seasoned salt
1	teaspoon garlic salt
1	teaspoon poultry seasoning
4	eggs
1	bottle (14¾ ounces) Stroh Ranch Smoky Jalapeño Honey Sauce, Hot or Mild to taste

Preheat oven to 325 degrees. Sauté onions in butter until soft. Combine onions, turkey, stuffing, salt, seasoned salt, garlic salt, poultry seasoning, and eggs in a large bowl. Roll mixture into walnut size balls. Fry balls in a small amount of butter until browned or bake on a greased baking sheet at 325 degrees for 15 minutes until done. Transfer meatballs to a 13x9x2-inch baking dish. Pour on Stroh Ranch Smoky Jalapeño Honey Sauce. Stir meatballs until well coated. Reheat meatballs until thoroughly heated. Serve in a hot dish with toothpicks.

Mom had fun coming up with this recipe to serve with our Stroh Ranch Smoky Jalapeño Honey Sauces (see www.pjsgourmet.com). This recipe shows our sauce so well. The meatballs are labor intensive, but well worth the time. They taste the best if you can keep them warm while serving.

25

COUNTRY COOKING

Beef Meatballs with Apricot Glaze   Yields: 40 meatballs

Meatballs

1½	**pounds lean ground beef**
2	**eggs**
2	**tablespoons dried parsley**
1	**package (1 ounce) dry onion soup mix**
2	**tablespoons water**
¼	**cup dry seasoned stuffing mix, crushed**
¼	**cup butter**

Apricot Glaze

1	**cup apricot jam**
¼	**cup ketchup**
Dash of wine vinegar	

Combine ground beef, eggs, parsley, onion mix, water, and stuffing in a bowl. Roll mixture into walnut size balls. Fry in a small amount of butter until browned. Transfer meatballs to a 13x9x2-inch baking dish. Combine jam, ketchup, and vinegar in a saucepan. Bring to boil. Pour glaze over meatballs. Stir meatballs until coated. Reheat meatballs at 350 degrees until thoroughly heated. Serve hot with toothpicks.

My Grandma Stroh shared this one with my Mom long ago. My daughter and husband love these meatballs especially with the sweet apricot glaze over them.

26

APPETIZERS

Cream Puffs

Yields: 48 cream puffs

1   cup water
½   cup butter
1   cup all-purpose flour
4   eggs

Preheat oven to 350 degrees. Bring water and butter to boil in a medium saucepan. Whisk in flour and cook until mixture forms a ball. Transfer to a mixing bowl. Slowly beat in eggs, one at a time, until well blended. Drop dough by teaspoonfuls onto a baking sheet. Bake 25 minutes or until puffy and golden browned. Cool completely. Slice open one edge and fill with Country-Style Turkey Salad *(see page 93)* or East-West Sausage *(see page 4)*.

This is one of my favorite appetizers. Mom would stuff them with the East-West Sausage. When she opened up the catering business, the Country-Style Turkey Salad recipe became a big hit too! You can even stuff them with your favorite egg salad recipe.

27

Baked Spinach and Bacon Dip

Serves: 10

1 **package (10 ounces) frozen chopped spinach, thawed and squeezed dry**

1 **cup mayonnaise**

1 **package (8 ounces) cream cheese, softened**

1 **small yellow onion, minced**

2 **garlic cloves, minced**

1 **cup grated Parmesan cheese**

1/8 **teaspoon pepper**

1 **pound bacon, cooked and crumbled**

2 **tablespoons grated Parmesan cheese**

Baguette slices or assorted crackers

Preheat oven to 350 degrees. Combine spinach, mayonnaise, cream cheese, onions, garlic, Parmesan cheese, pepper, and bacon in a large bowl. Spread mixture evenly into a quiche dish. Sprinkle Parmesan cheese on top. Bake 30 minutes or until hot in center and lightly browned. Serve hot with baguette slices or crackers.

I was so happy to find this recipe. Mom served this many times, but I had always forgotten to write it down. She served it hot in a chafing dish with an assortment of crackers and slices of baguette. Sometimes she would add more garlic because she loved lots of garlic in everything.

Basil Torte

Serves: 12

Cheese Filling

1   cup low-fat ricotta cheese
**4   ounces light cream cheese,
      softened**
Cheesecloth

Pesto Filling

**2½ cups tightly packed fresh
      basil leaves**
**1   cup freshly grated
      Parmesan cheese**
1   tablespoon olive oil
1   large garlic clove
1-2 tablespoons water
¼   cup pine nuts
Salt to taste
Basil sprigs for garnish
**Assorted crackers, bread or
      vegetables**

Beat ricotta cheese and cream cheese with an electric mixer in a small bowl until well blended. Set aside. Smoothly line a deep, round glass mold with a double layer of moistened and wrung-dry cheesecloth. Cloth should drape over rim. Blend basil, Parmesan cheese, olive oil, garlic, and enough water in a food processor to make a smooth paste. Pour pesto mixture into a bowl. Stir in pine nuts and salt. Set aside. With a spoon, press one-fourth cheese filling evenly into the bottom of the mold. Spread one-third of pesto filling over the cheese. Repeat layers, ending with a layer of cheese. Fold edges of cheesecloth smoothly over cheese. Tightly cover with plastic wrap. Refrigerate at least 2 hours or until next day. Fold back the cloth and invert torte onto a small platter. Gently lift off the cheesecloth. Garnish top with basil sprigs. Serve with crackers, bread, or vegetables.

This is a beautiful and wonderfully rich appetizer. This was one of Mom's first appetizers that she made for the catering business.

COUNTRY COOKING

Crab Mousse with Stroh Ranch Marinade   Serves: 10

1 **can (10¾ ounces) cream of mushroom soup**

1 **package (8 ounces) cream cheese**

2 **tablespoons unflavored gelatin**

¼ **cup warm water**

8 **ounces fresh cooked crabmeat, minced or use imitation crabmeat**

¼ **cup minced green onions**

1 **cup mayonnaise**

¼ **cup Stroh Ranch Original Marinade, well shaken**

Assorted crackers

Heat soup and cream cheese until melted. Dissolve gelatin in water. Add gelatin mixture to soup and mix thoroughly. Pour into a bowl. Add crabmeat, green onions, mayonnaise, and marinade. Mix well. Pour mixture into a large mold lined with plastic wrap. Refrigerate until chilled. Invert the mousse onto your favorite platter. Serve with crackers.

Here is another one of Mom's creations that uses our Stroh Ranch Original Marinade (see www.pjsgourmet.com). This recipe is the most popular at my food tasting events. I sell more marinade because of this recipe than any other recipe that has our marinade in it. The marinade gives the mousse a smoky flavor unlike any crab mousse we know, and people love it!

30

APPETIZERS

Winter Pears with Blue Cheese

Serves: 12

4   **Comice pears**

4   **ounces blue cheese, softened**

1   **package (8 ounces) cream cheese, softened**

Milk

Pastry bag

Slice each pear in half lengthwise. Remove center with seeds. Place the cut side down and thinly slice lengthwise. Blend blue cheese and cream cheese in a food processor. Add enough milk to make a creamy and smooth consistency. Spoon mixture into the pastry bag with a wide tip. With the pear slices laying flat on a serving dish, pipe a small amount onto each pear slice and serve immediately.

I learned about this recipe when I worked at a winery in the Napa Valley. One of the caterers had it at an event, and I loved it. I told Mom about it and she recreated it perfectly without the original recipe. She served the slices on a huge, beautiful metal platter shaped like a pear.

31

Marinated Chicken Wings

Serves: 6

16 **cocktail chicken wings**
¼ **bottle (12.7 ounces) Stroh Ranch Original Marinade**

Preheat oven to 350 degrees. Place chicken wings in a baking dish. Bake until done. Drain the juices. Pour marinade over wings and toss to coat. Bake an additional 5-10 minutes to allow the marinade to bake into the chicken. Drain. Serve immediately on a platter.

Mom came up with this easy and very tasty recipe to share with our customers. The marinade (see www.pjsgourmet.com) makes any cut of chicken delicious.

32

Blue Cheese Nibbles

Serves: 6

6 tablespoons butter

1¼ cups crumbled blue cheese

1 package (16 ounces) refrigerated jumbo biscuits

Preheat oven to 350 degrees. Melt butter in the bottom of a quiche dish in the oven. Sprinkle blue cheese evenly on the bottom of the dish. On a cutting board, cut each biscuit into 3 wedges. Arrange the 24 biscuit pieces over the cheese. Bake 25 minutes or until golden browned and cooked through. Serve in the dish with a small spatula.

Mom created this one — I remember the day. I ate so many of these that I could barely eat dinner!

33

Rumaki

Serves: 8

Rumaki

1½ pounds thick slice bacon
1 can (8 ounces) water chestnuts, drained
Toothpicks

Sauce

1 cup ketchup
½ cup Dijon mustard
½ cup packed brown sugar

Preheat oven to 350 degrees. Cut bacon slices in half. Cut the larger water chestnuts in half. Wrap chestnut in bacon slices. Secure through the top with a toothpick. Place seam side down on a broiler pan. Bake 45 minutes or until the bacon is thoroughly cooked and lightly browned. Combine ketchup, mustard, and brown sugar in a saucepan. Cook and stir until hot. Pour sauce into a small bowl and place on a platter with the rumaki. Serve both warm and don't forget a small bowl for the used toothpicks.

Whenever our birthdays came around, Mom always granted us the menu of our choice for dinner — from appetizers to dessert. This is the appetizer I always chose. It was always a treat to have bacon!

Bean Dip

Serves: 10

1   **can (15 ounces) chili with beans**

1   **can (15 ounces) chili without beans**

2   **packages (8 ounces each) cream cheese**

Tortilla chips

Combine chili with beans, chili without beans, and cream cheese in a saucepan. Cook and stir over low heat until cheese melts and mixture is thoroughly heated. Serve hot in a ceramic bowl with tortilla chips.

This was very popular with our customers all year long. I remember Mom making this long ago for our family. Sometimes we would add a little hot pepper sauce.

35

Endive and Shrimp

Serves: 10

1 **package (8 ounces) cream cheese, softened**
½ **cup mayonnaise**
1 **tablespoon minced fresh dill**
¼ **teaspoon salt**
2 **cups cooked baby shrimp**
4 **heads of endive, in season**

Blend cream cheese, mayonnaise, dill, and salt in a bowl. Gently squeeze shrimp to remove extra water. Stir shrimp into cream cheese mixture. Cut the bottom end off the head of endive and pull off the loose leaves. Cut the end again and continue to pull off the loose leaves until you reach the core. Spoon a small amount of shrimp mixture onto the white end of the endive. Arrange on a platter and refrigerate until ready to serve.

Mom always enjoyed serving this recipe to her customers. It looks beautiful on a glass platter. It is important to buy the endive in season otherwise it may taste bitter. Curly endive is the variety my mom used. It is available at its peak from June through October. Belgian endive is available September through May but it is more bitter than the curly endive.

APPETIZERS

Fruit Dip

Yields: 1¾ cups

1   container (8 ounces) sour cream
½   cup packed brown sugar
2   tablespoons coffee-flavored liqueur
1   teaspoon vanilla
1   container (8 ounces) frozen whipped topping, thawed
Sliced fruit

Combine sour cream, brown sugar, liqueur, vanilla, and whipped topping in a bowl. Cover and refrigerate. It is important the brown sugar has been mixed in thoroughly. Serve as a dipping sauce for sliced or chunked fresh fruit or fruit kabobs.

What an amazing fruit dip! Mom always served this as an appetizer during her summer jobs with fresh fruit. She enjoyed serving it with a huge bowl of strawberries. She would place a small glass bowl with a pedestal inside of a glass punch bowl. She filled the small glass bowl with the dip and surrounded it with strawberries. We think this dip is better than dipping fruit into chocolate! You could use this recipe as a dessert too and serve over brownies and pie. It would also be great in the morning on your coffee.

37

Stuffed Mushrooms   Serves: 8

24 ounces medium whole mushrooms

1 package (8 ounces) cream cheese, softened

⅓ pound ham, minced

Preheat oven to 350 degrees. Remove mushroom stems. Blend cream cheese and ham. Using a small spoon, stuff mushroom caps with filling and place on a baking sheet. Bake on middle rack 20 minutes or until mushrooms are soft to the touch and steaming.

This was the second most popular appetizer that Mom served next to Jeanette's Garlic Dip. These mushrooms are very addicting and so simple to make. Sometimes Mom would use black forest ham, but most of the time she would buy a large ham roast. She would cut it into chunks and mince the amount she needed in a food processor and freeze leftover.

Layered Crab Dip

Serves: 10

1   **package (8 ounces) cream cheese, softened**
2   **tablespoons lemon juice**
2   **tablespoons mayonnaise**
$\frac{1}{2}$ **teaspoon seasoned salt**
$\frac{1}{2}$ **teaspoon Worcestershire sauce**
$\frac{1}{2}$ **bottle (12 ounces) cocktail sauce**
1   **pound shredded cooked crabmeat**
1   **package (8 ounces) shredded Monterey Jack cheese**
1   **can (2.25 ounces) sliced black olives**
$\frac{1}{4}$ **cup sliced green onions**
Assorted crackers or baguette slices

Blend cream cheese, lemon juice, mayonnaise, salt, and Worcestershire sauce in a food processor. Spread mixture on the bottom of a platter with 1-inch sides. Pour cocktail sauce evenly over cream cheese mixture. Sprinkle crabmeat evenly over cocktail sauce. Sprinkle three-fourths Jack cheese over crab. Top with black olives and green onions. Sprinkle remaining cheese on top. Refrigerate. Serve with crackers or baguette slices.

Mary Louise Chase, a close family friend, shared this wonderful recipe with Mom. Everyone loved this beautiful and delicious dip. Mom served it in a hand-made ceramic platter with a variety of crackers.

39

Chile Frittata

Serves: 10

¼ **cup butter**

½ **cup all-purpose flour**

½ **teaspoon salt**

10 **eggs, beaten**

1 **package (12 ounces) shredded Cheddar cheese**

1 **can (7 ounces) chopped green chilies**

1 **cup small curd cottage cheese**

Preheat oven to 350 degrees. Melt butter in a 13x9x2-inch baking dish in the oven. Combine flour, salt, eggs, cheese, chilies, and cottage cheese in a bowl and mix well. Pour mixture over butter. Bake 25 minutes or until golden browned. Cool to warm and cut into small squares.

This was another favorite appetizer of Jeanette's Country Cooking. Once you pop one in your mouth, you won't be able to stop! This recipe can also be used as a side dish with a main course.

40

Spinach and Artichoke Dip

Serves: 8

1 **package (10 ounces) frozen chopped spinach, thawed and squeezed dry**

1 **jar (6 ounces) marinated artichoke hearts, drained and quartered**

1 **cup grated Parmesan cheese**

1 **cup mayonnaise**

1 **can (4 ounces) diced green chilies**

Tortilla chips

Preheat oven to 350 degrees. Combine spinach, artichoke hearts, Parmesan cheese, mayonnaise, and green chilies in a bowl. Pour mixture into a quiche pan. Bake 30 minutes or until golden browned. Use a paper towel to soak up any extra oil on top before serving. Serve hot with tortilla chips.

Thanks to our close family friend, Kay Hill, we have this delicious recipe. She gave it to Mom back in March of 1983. The green chilies really add to this recipe. My tasters loved this one!

41

COUNTRY COOKING

Blue Cheese Pear

Serves: 8

1 **package (8 ounces) shredded sharp Cheddar cheese, room temperature**

1 **package (3 ounces) cream cheese, softened**

½ **cup crumbled blue cheese, room temperature**

½ **cup finely chopped walnuts**

1 **garlic clove, crushed**

Cinnamon stick for garnish

Mint leaves for garnish

Paprika for garnish

Assorted crackers or fruit

Blend Cheddar cheese, cream cheese, blue cheese, walnuts, and garlic in food processor until smooth. If necessary, add a few teaspoons milk to reach a smooth consistency. Shape cheese mixture into a pear shape. Place cinnamon stick in through the top as a stem. Add at least 3 mint leaves at the stem. Pat the paprika on sides of the pear to create a shadow. Cover and refrigerate. Let stand at room temperature for 30 minutes before serving. Serve with crackers and fruit.

This recipe was featured in an article that Country America *magazine had written about Mom in January of 1993. The pear looks beautiful on a glass plate served with sliced apples and crackers.*

42

Curry Bites

Serves: 10

5 **English muffins**

2 **tablespoons chopped black olives**

3 **green onions, minced, green part only**

1 **package (8 ounces) shredded Cheddar cheese**

¾ **cup mayonnaise**

2½ **teaspoons curry powder**

Preheat oven to 350 degrees. Split English muffins in half and toast until golden browned. When cool, cut the 10 halves into quarters, making 40 wedges. Combine black olives, green onions, cheese, mayonnaise, and curry in a small bowl. Spoon a generous layer onto each muffin wedge. Place on a baking sheet. Bake 15 minutes or until cheese melts and is bubbly. Serve warm on a platter.

This is a great recipe from my childhood. I loved curry then and even more now. Mom made these when we had company over and then served them at catering jobs when Jeanette's Country Cooking started.

43

Spinach and Cottage Cheese Bites

Serves: 8

1   **package (10 ounces) frozen chopped spinach, thawed and squeezed dry**
6   **eggs, beaten**
½   **cup butter, cut up**
1   **package (8 ounces) shredded sharp Cheddar cheese**
2   **pounds small curd cottage cheese**
6   **tablespoons all-purpose flour**

Preheat oven to 350 degrees. Combine spinach, eggs, butter, Cheddar cheese, cottage cheese, and flour. Spoon mixture into a greased 13x9x2-inch baking dish. Bake 1 hour or until browned. Cool to warm and cut into squares.

Our close friend, Gary Venturi, shared this one with Mom when he was the innkeeper for La Chaumiere Bed and Breakfast in Calistoga. Mom and Dad enjoyed these when they arrived for their 2 day vacation from the ranch. She loved every recipe of Gary's! These were a hit at one of our dinner parties. We even enjoyed them for breakfast the next morning! It is important to use the small curd cottage cheese so the ingredients bind better. It might be fun to also try the recipe with chopped broccoli or chopped zucchini.

44

Hearts of Palm Dip

Yields: 2 cups for 20 people

1 cup sour cream
1 cup mayonnaise
2 garlic cloves, crushed
1 ½ teaspoons salt
1 ½ teaspoons steak sauce
1 ½ teaspoons Worcestershire sauce
2 drops hot pepper sauce
1 ½ teaspoons dried parsley
2 green onions, minced
1 ½ teaspoons lemon juice
2 cans (14 ½ ounces each) hearts of palm, sliced into ¾-inch pieces

Combine sour cream, mayonnaise, garlic, salt, steak sauce, Worcestershire sauce, hot pepper sauce, parsley, onions, and lemon juice in a small bowl. Arrange hearts of palm slices on a platter. Spoon a small amount of dip on each slice. Refrigerate until ready to serve.

The hearts of palm taste wonderful with this very flavorful dip. My sister, Kathy, and I used the extra dip that was leftover with tortilla chips and everyone enjoyed the dip all over again.

45

Marinated Mushrooms

Serves: 8

- ½ **teaspoon lemon juice**
- ½ **teaspoon salt**
- 12 **ounces baby brown pearl mushrooms**
- 2 **tablespoons lemon juice**
- 1¼ **teaspoons salt**
- ⅓ **cup olive oil**
- ¼ **teaspoon pepper**
- 1 **garlic clove**
- 1 **bay leaf**
- 1 **teaspoon dried oregano**

In a small pot, bring water to a boil with the lemon juice and salt. Add mushrooms and boil 1 minute. Drain mushrooms and immerse into cold water until cool. Drain and set aside. Combine lemon juice, salt, oil, pepper, garlic, bay leaf, and oregano in a small bowl. Pour marinade into a plastic container with a tight fitting lid. Add mushrooms and marinate overnight. Shake the container occasionally while marinating. Serve in a small bowl with toothpicks.

I tried this recipe on my in-laws, Jack and Nancy Reardan, and my brother-in-law's family, Brad and Espy Reardan, and nephews Michael and Cesar. They all loved it. I enjoyed the tang of the lemon and the spice of the oregano together. It was easy to make and looks pretty in a glass bowl with fancy toothpicks.

46

Cream Cheese and Vegetable Spread   Serves: 10

4 **radishes, halved**

4 **green onions, cut into 1-inch pieces**

½ **small cucumber, peeled, seeded and cut into 4 pieces**

½ **stick celery, cut into 1-inch pieces**

⅔ **bell pepper, cut into 4 pieces**

1 **package (8 ounces) cream cheese, cut into 8 pieces**

1 **tablespoon sour cream**

½ **teaspoon salt**

¼ **teaspoon pepper**

Assorted crackers or baguettes slices

Combine radishes, green onions, cucumbers, celery, and peppers in a food processor. Pulse off and on until all vegetables are evenly chopped. Add cream cheese, sour cream, salt, and pepper and process until thoroughly mixed but still chunky. Cover and refrigerate. Serve in a decorative bowl with crackers or baguette slices.

We enjoyed testing this recipe with water biscuits that are flavorless so the natural flavor of this delicious dip can be appreciated. It would be best made a day ahead to let the flavors marry. A large food processor works best. If you do not have one, I would suggest mincing all the vegetables to the same size.

Salsa and Cream Cheese

Serves: 8

1 package (8 ounces) cream cheese, softened
1 bottle (24 ounces) chipotle salsa
Tortilla chips

Spread cream cheese evenly on the bottom of a decorative shallow bowl. Pour salsa on top and cover with plastic wrap. Place in the microwave for 2 to 3 minutes until heated through. Serve warm with your favorite tortilla chips.

This is one of my favorite appetizers to serve last minute. Everyone loves it, and it is so easy. Chipotle-style salsas are the best, but any red salsa would taste great. The bowl I use is 10-inches in diameter and 2-inches deep.

Breads
&
Brunch

CONTENTS

Whipping Cream Biscuits

Yields: 24 biscuits

1 ½ teaspoons sugar
2 cups all-purpose flour
1 tablespoon baking powder
1 teaspoon salt
¼ cup butter, cut into small pieces
1 cup plus 2 tablespoons heavy cream

Preheat oven to 425 degrees. Combine sugar, flour, baking powder, and salt. Cut in butter until mixture resembles coarse meal. Add cream and stir with a fork until moistened. Immediately turn out onto a lightly floured board. Knead the dough a few times. Roll dough flat into a 12-inch diameter round circle. Cut dough with a 2-inch biscuit cutter. Bake 15 minutes or until golden browned.

This is one of Pat Denny's recipes. We enjoyed testing them over Easter weekend with family. They were great hot out of the oven with lots of butter on top!

51

Sweet Dinner Rolls

Yields: 15 rolls

1 **cup warm water**
1 **package (0.25 ounce) active dry yeast**
¼ **cup canola oil**
1 **egg**
½ **teaspoon salt**
¼ **cup sugar**
3¾ **cups all-purpose flour**

Combine warm water and yeast in a large bowl. Beat together oil and egg in a separate bowl. Add egg mixture to yeast. Add salt, sugar, and flour and mix well. The dough will be slightly sticky. Spoon dough onto a floured board. Knead dough five times until dough is not so sticky. Place dough ball back into large bowl. Place bowl in a warm place. Cover with a towel. Let rise for 30 minutes. Grease cups in a muffin pan (do not use paper cups). Using floured hands, roll the dough into 1-inch balls. Place three balls into the bottom of each muffin cup. Bake at 350 degrees 15-20 minutes or until the rolls are golden browned. Serve warm.

I'm so happy to have this sweet yeast roll recipe in the cookbook. Butter is all you need to serve these to your family and friends. I have our friends, Barbara Hopper and Jim Eddie, to thank. Jim shared the recipe with Barbara who shared it for the cookbook in honor of Mom. The rolls turn out beautifully and are easy to pull apart.

Coffee Can Bread   Serves: 8

1   package (0.25 ounce) active
    dry yeast
½   cup warm water
¼   teaspoon ground ginger
3   tablespoons sugar
1   can (12 ounces) evaporated
    milk
1   teaspoon salt
2   tablespoons vegetable oil
4½ cups all-purpose flour

Combine yeast and warm water in a bowl. Let stand 5 minutes. Add ginger, sugar, milk, salt, oil, and flour and mix well. The dough will be very sticky. Oil a 2-pound coffee can. Be sure to take the plastic label off the front of the can if there is one. Press dough into the can and oil the plastic top. Place the top loosely on the coffee can and leave in a warm place (outside in the sun or in a warm oven) for 2 hours or until the top pops off. Bake at 350 degrees for 60 minutes. If using 1-pound cans, bake for 45 minutes. Cool 10 minutes. Try to pop the bread out of the can by shaking it slightly. If it does not pop out, open the opposite end with a can opener and push the bread out. Serve warm with butter.

This is my dad's favorite! It is heavy textured bread and great toasted or used for sandwiches the next day.

53

Homemade French Bread

Yields: 2 loaves

Sourdough Starter

1   package (0.25 ounce) active dry yeast

1½ cups warm water

1   tablespoon sugar

1½ cups all-purpose flour

French Bread

1   package (0.25 ounce) active dry yeast

1½ cups warm water

1   cup starter dough

6   cups all-purpose flour

2   teaspoons salt

2½ teaspoons sugar

½   teaspoon baking soda

Combine yeast, water, sugar, and flour and pour into a crockpot. Let stand in a warm place for 5 days, stirring occasionally. Place starter in refrigerator until ready to make bread. Dissolve yeast in water. Stir in starter. Add 4½ cups flour, salt, and sugar. Cover and let rise in a warm place for 2-3 hours. Mix baking soda with 1 cup of flour. Stir into dough. Knead on a floured board for 10 minutes. Shape dough into 2 loaves. Cover lightly and let rise 2 hours. Brush loaves with water. Slice diagonal cuts into the tops of loaves. Place bread in a shallow pan. Place pan in a larger pan with hot water covering the bottom. Bake at 400 degrees for 45 minutes.

Note: This recipe takes 5 days to make.

My Grandma Stroh, who was raised in San Francisco, shared this recipe with Mom. Notes on the recipe say it yields San Francisco-style bread. My tasters loved this bread. I knew this recipe was made many times because of the dough and torn edges on the recipe sheet. It was hard to wait the 5 days, but well worth it.

54

French Bread with Mayonnaise, Parmesan and Green Onions

Serves: 8

1	**loaf sourdough French bread**
2	**cups mayonnaise**
2	**cups grated Parmesan cheese**
3	**green onions, trimmed and minced**

Slice the French bread in half lengthwise. Combine mayonnaise, Parmesan cheese, and green onions. Spread mixture evenly over two bread halves. Place bread, one at a time, in the middle of the oven under the broiler. Broil bread 5 minutes or until the top is golden browned and heated through. Slice bread and serve warm.

Our family thought it was such a treat when Mom served this recipe to us. The topping is so rich and yummy! Knowing what I know now about calories, I can understand why Mom didn't serve this to us more often.

55

Basic Garlic Bread

Serves: 8

1   **loaf sourdough French bread**
¾   **cup butter or margarine**
6   **garlic cloves, chopped**

Slice bread in half lengthwise. Combine butter and garlic in a saucepan. Sauté gently. Spoon garlic butter evenly over bread halves. Broil until golden browned. Slice and serve warm.

This has always been a favorite of our family. The broiling is what makes it delicious and crunchy. The best bread we found to use is pugliese (pronounced poo-lyeh-sey). It is a wonderful Italian bread with lots of yeast flavor and not too thick.

56

Mrs. Moon's Pizza Crust

Serves: 6

1 package (0.25 ounce) active dry yeast
2 tablespoons warm water
1 egg
1 tablespoon sugar
1 teaspoon salt
1 tablespoon vegetable oil
1 cup warm water
3 cups all-purpose flour

Combine yeast and warm water in a cup and set aside. Beat egg in a large bowl. Add sugar, salt, and oil. Mix thoroughly. Slowly stir in warm water and add yeast mixture. Mix in flour. Knead dough on a floured board until rubbery. Place dough on an oiled pizza pan. With floured hands, press dough to within one-inch of the edge of the pizza pan. Let rise in a warm place for 30 minutes. Add your favorite toppings and bake at 425 degrees for 30 minutes.

This recipe came from Mom's close friend, Karen Moon. Karen would bring her entire third grade class to the catering kitchen on the ranch as a field trip to make individual pizzas with this dough and bake cookies and eat slices of watermelon. The students had so much fun and looked so cute with their aprons on and flour all over them.

Golden Corn Bread

Serves: 8

1½ cups yellow cornmeal
1 teaspoon salt
1 teaspoon baking soda
1 tablespoon sugar
2 cups buttermilk
1 egg
2 tablespoons vegetable oil
1 cup shredded Cheddar cheese

Preheat oven to 400 degrees. Combine cornmeal, salt, baking soda, and sugar. Add buttermilk, egg, and oil. Mix well. Blend in cheese. Pour batter into a greased 8x8x2-inch baking dish. Bake 20 minutes or until golden browned. Serve warm with butter.

My Grandma Stroh gave this one to Mom. It comes out rich and moist and not too sweet.

58

Yorkshire Pudding   Serves: 6

1   cup all-purpose flour
3/4 teaspoon salt
2   large eggs
1   cup milk
1   tablespoon vegetable oil

Preheat oven to 450 degrees. In a small bowl combine by hand flour, salt, eggs, and milk until well blended. Pour oil into a 13x9x2-inch baking dish. Heat dish in the oven until hot. Pour batter into dish. Place on top rack of oven. Bake about 30 minutes or until well-risen and golden browned. Serve with your favorite beef roast with lots of gravy on top.

Mom loved this recipe that I found long ago. The pudding is so much fun to watch baking. It bubbles up very high and then settles down slightly when you take it out of the oven. It is definitely a conversation piece!

59

Brown Nut Bread

Yields: 1 loaf

**1 ½ cups sour milk
(add 2 tablespoons
vinegar to milk)**
½ cup molasses
2 cups graham flour
1 teaspoon baking soda
1 teaspoon baking powder
½ cup chopped walnuts
Salt to taste

Preheat oven to 350 degrees. Combine milk, molasses, flour, baking soda, baking powder, walnuts, and salt. Pour batter into a greased 9x5-inch loaf pan. Bake for 55 minutes.

My "Grandma #3", Kay Whittaker, shared this recipe in honor of Mom. Kay and her husband, Ralph, were our neighbors for many years. We were so sad when they moved to Tonopah, Nevada but have continued to keep in close contact. She told me it is a very old recipe that her sister, Eva Moody, had made long ago. It is a dense bread and flavorful with the molasses and walnuts. We enjoyed it toasted the next day with butter and jam.

Pineapple and Carrot Bread

Yields: 2 loaves

3   **eggs**
1½ **cups vegetable oil**
2   **cups sugar**
1   **can (8.25 ounces) crushed pineapple**
2   **cups finely grated carrots**
3   **teaspoons vanilla**
3   **cups all-purpose flour**
3   **tablespoons cinnamon**
1   **teaspoon salt**
1   **teaspoon baking soda**

Preheat oven to 325 degrees. Combine eggs, oil, sugar, pineapple, carrots, vanilla, flour, cinnamon, salt, and baking soda. Beat well. Pour batter into two greased 9x5-inch loaf pans. Bake 50 minutes or until the tops spring back upon touching them.

If you like cinnamon, you will love this bread. It was fun to find this recipe. Mom gave it to Pat Denny back in 1971. A note on the back of the recipe stated this recipe is "extremely good and moist. I've won first prize at the fair for 3 years with it! Hope you like it."

Prune Bread

Serves: 12

1   **cup pitted prunes, diced**
1   **cup vegetable oil**
4   **eggs**
2   **cups sugar**
1   **cup chopped nuts**
2   **cups all-purpose flour**
1   **teaspoon cinnamon**
1   **teaspoon ground nutmeg**
1   **teaspoon ground cloves**
1   **teaspoon baking soda**
1   **teaspoon ground allspice**
1   **teaspoon salt**
1   **teaspoon baking powder**
½   **cup buttermilk**
½   **cup sherry**

Preheat oven to 325 degrees. Combine prunes, oil, eggs, sugar, nuts, flour, cinnamon, nutmeg, cloves, baking soda, allspice, salt, baking powder, milk, and sherry in a large bowl. Pour batter into a greased tube pan. Bake for 1 hour, 30 minutes.

Thankfully our close family friend, Carole Stokes, found this recipe that Mom had written out for her many years ago. Mom had a note on this recipe that Dad loves it. It is a moist cake with a wonderful spice flavor.

BREADS & BRUNCH

Banana Bread

Yields: 2 loaves

2	**cups sugar**
1	**cup vegetable oil**
4	**eggs**
5	**large very ripe bananas, puréed**
2	**teaspoons vanilla**
4	**cups all-purpose flour**
2	**teaspoons baking soda**
4	**teaspoons baking powder**
1	**cup milk**

Preheat oven to 350 degrees. In a large bowl, cream sugar and oil. Stir in eggs, bananas, and vanilla until blended. In a separate bowl, combine flour, baking soda, and baking powder. Add flour mixture and milk to creamed mixture and mix well. Divide batter between two greased 9x5-inch loaf pans. Bake about 40 minutes or until a toothpick inserted comes out clean.

This is my banana bread recipe that I am sharing in honor of Mom. I have worked on this one over the years and finally perfected it. Our family loves banana bread. We purposely let our bananas get overripe and stick them in a plastic bag in the freezer. When the time comes to make the bread, we just pull the bananas from the freezer, thaw them and start cooking. Using very ripe bananas will give you the best flavor. If you are in a hurry, just ask your local grocery store for their overripe bananas that are probably in the warehouse somewhere. We love toasting the bread and spreading butter and homemade wild blackberry jam on every slice.

63

Zucchini Bread

Yields: 2 loaves

3   **eggs**
1   **cup vegetable oil**
2   **cups sugar**
2   **cups grated zucchini**
2   **teaspoons vanilla**
1   **teaspoon salt**
1   **teaspoon baking soda**
1   **teaspoon cinnamon**
½   **teaspoon baking powder**
3   **cups all-purpose flour**
1   **cup chopped walnuts (optional)**

Preheat oven to 325 degrees. In a large bowl, cream eggs, oil, and sugar. Add zucchini and vanilla and mix well. In a separate bowl, combine salt, baking soda, cinnamon, baking powder, and flour. Add flour mixture to egg mixture and mix well. Pour batter into two oiled and floured 9x5-inch loaf pans. Bake for 1 hour.

Like everyone else, we always had too much zucchini when we grew it on the ranch. We always knew Mom would make zucchini bread. That was the only way we would eat it!

64

Pear Bread

Yields: 1 loaf

½ **cup butter, room temperature**

1½ **cups sugar**

2 **eggs**

2 **cups mashed ripe pears**

2 **cups all-purpose flour**

2 **teaspoons baking soda**

2 **teaspoons cinnamon**

1 **teaspoon salt**

½ **teaspoon ground cloves**

½ **teaspoon ground nutmeg**

Preheat oven to 350 degrees. Cream butter and sugar. Add eggs, pears, flour, baking soda, cinnamon, salt, cloves, and nutmeg. Pour batter into a 9x5-inch loaf pan. Bake for 45-50 minutes.

The spices really complement the pears in this recipe. Potter Valley is known for excellent Bartlett pears so this recipe was always enjoyed during the summer pear season. I suggest using very ripe pears for added flavor.

65

Golden Cinnamon Rolls

Yields: 36 rolls

Cinnamon Rolls

2½ cups warm water

2 packages (0.25 ounce each) active dry yeast

1 package (18.25 ounces) yellow cake mix

4½ cups all-purpose flour

Filling

½ cup butter, melted

1 cup sugar

4 teaspoons cinnamon

1 cup dried cranberries (optional)

1 cup chopped nuts (optional)

Icing

3 cups powdered sugar

4 tablespoons butter, melted

4 tablespoons milk

Mix water and yeast together in a large bowl. Stir in cake mix and flour until completely combined. Let dough rise in a warm place until doubled in size. Divide dough in half. Roll first half onto a large floured board to a 16x12-inch rectangle. Continually flour the board so the dough does not stick to the board. For the filling, spread half melted butter evenly over each dough rectangle. Sprinkle ½ cup sugar evenly over each dough rectangle. Sprinkle 2 teaspoons cinnamon evenly over each rectangle. Sprinkle ½ cup dried cranberries and ½ cup nuts evenly over each dough rectangle. Roll each dough rectangle into a long roll starting from the long side. Slice into 18 pieces. Place slices flat and evenly spaced on a large, non-perforated pizza pan. To bake right away, let rolls rise for 15 minutes in a warm place. Bake at 350 degrees for 20 minutes or until golden browned. To make the next morning, cover with plastic wrap and refrigerate overnight. In the morning, set pans at room temperature for 10 minutes. Preheat oven to 350 degrees. Bake about 20 minutes or until golden browned. For the icing, blend powdered sugar, butter, and milk. Spread one teaspoon icing on baked cinnamon rolls. Serve rolls warm or at room temperature.

This is a unique recipe that came from our close family friend, Barbara Hopper, who shared this recipe in honor of Mom. I use non-perforated pizza pans so the rolls will stay round instead of using a baking sheet where the sides may become flat. I tested them without the cranberries and nuts. Either way, you will love them!

"Catering is loads of fun. I love it. It's challenging, and I guess you have to have a sense of humor along with this to keep your sanity sometimes, but I love to cook."

Jeanette Stroh
September 1991

67

Cinnamon Cake

Serves: 6

Cake

1 ⅓ cups biscuit baking mix
¾ cup milk
¾ cup sugar
1 teaspoon vanilla
1 egg
⅓ cup vegetable oil
1 teaspoon cinnamon

Topping

¼ cup all-purpose flour
¼ cup sugar
1 tablespoon cinnamon
¼ cup margarine

Preheat oven to 350 degrees. Combine baking mix, milk, sugar, vanilla, egg, oil, and cinnamon. Pour batter into a greased 8x8x2-inch baking dish. For the topping, mix together flour, sugar, and cinnamon. Cut in margarine until crumbly with a coarse consistency. Sprinkle on top. Bake for 35 minutes.

Our family has always loved cinnamon in anything. This is easy to make and wonderful served hot in the morning.

Bacon and Egg Casserole

Serves: 8

16 hard-cooked eggs, very thinly sliced
1½ pounds bacon, cooked, drained and crumbled
¼ cup butter
¼ cup all-purpose flour
2 cups half-and-half
¼ teaspoon dried thyme
¼ teaspoon dried marjoram
¼ teaspoon dried basil
1 cup grated Cheddar cheese
¼ cup bread crumbs

Preheat oven to 350 degrees. Lightly toss eggs and bacon together in a small bowl. Spread mixture evenly in the bottom of a buttered 13x9x2-inch baking dish. Melt butter in a saucepan. Whisk in flour until thickened. Stir in half-and-half without thickening the mixture. Remove from heat. Add thyme, marjoram, basil, and Cheddar cheese. Mix well. Pour cheese sauce over egg and bacon mixture. Top with bread crumbs. Bake 30 minutes or until bubbly.

Supper Club members Judy and Larry Artman shared this favorite recipe of theirs in honor of Mom. It is a rich and flavorful breakfast dish. I enjoy the uniqueness of a breakfast casserole with hard-cooked eggs. This recipe has always been a part of the Artman's Christmas morning tradition. Judy suggests serving it with toasted English muffins and fresh fruit.

69

Mexican Egg Casserole

Serves: 8

½ cup all-purpose flour

1 teaspoon baking powder

12 eggs, lightly beaten

2 packages (8 ounces each) shredded Monterey Jack cheese

2 cups small-curd cottage cheese

2 plum tomatoes, seeded and diced

1 can (4 ounces) chopped green chilies, drained

4 green onions, sliced

½ teaspoon hot pepper sauce

1 teaspoon dried oregano

2 tablespoons minced fresh cilantro

½ teaspoon salt

½ teaspoon pepper

Salsa (optional)

Preheat oven to 400 degrees. In a large bowl, combine flour and baking powder. Add eggs, 3½ cups Monterey Jack cheese, cottage cheese, tomatoes, chilies, onions, hot pepper sauce, oregano, cilantro, salt, and pepper. Pour mixture into a greased 13x9x2-inch baking dish. Top with remaining Monterey Jack cheese. Bake, uncovered, for 15 minutes. Reduce heat to 350 degrees. Bake 30 minutes longer or until a knife inserted near the center comes out clean. Let stand for 5 minutes before cutting. Serve with salsa.

Your family and friends will enjoy this colorful and delicious casserole. Everyone I have served it to has loved it! We serve it with our favorite donuts and/or cinnamon rolls, coffee, and orange juice.

Roulade

Serves: 4

Roulade

1 ½ cups milk
4 tablespoons butter
3 tablespoons all-purpose flour
¼ teaspoon salt
⅛ teaspoon pepper
5 egg yolks, lightly beaten
5 egg whites
½ cup grated Parmesan cheese

Filling

1 packet (0.9 ounces) hollandaise sauce mix
1 cup milk
¼ cup butter
1 package (6 ounces) sliced ham
Fresh parsley, minced

Preheat oven to 350 degrees. Line a 15x10x3-inch baking sheet with parchment paper. Coat with cooking spray. Heat milk in a small saucepan over low heat until hot and set aside. To make the roux, melt butter in a medium saucepan. Whisk in flour until well dissolved. Whisk in heated milk, salt and pepper. Stir constantly until thickened. Add egg yolks to roux and stir constantly until incorporated. Set aside. In a separate bowl, beat egg whites until firm peaks form. Stir one-fourth egg whites and one-half Parmesan cheese into roux. Gently fold in remaining egg whites. Pour mixture into baking sheet and fill to the corners. Sprinkle remaining cheese on top. Bake about 15 minutes until puffy and lightly browned. Let cool. Invert roulade onto parchment paper. Remove top parchment paper. For the filling, whisk together hollandaise sauce mix and milk in a saucepan. Add butter and bring to boil, stirring frequently, until thickened. Set aside. Arrange ham slices along top of the long side of the roulade. Gently roll into a long roll and slice into 8 pieces. Place slices flat in a baking dish. Drizzle hollandaise sauce over top. Bake for another 10 minutes until thoroughly heated. Sprinkle with parsley and serve hot.

What a wonderful breakfast this makes! The Parmesan cheese adds to the richness of the roulade. It looks very pretty on a dish served with fresh fruit.

71

Sausage "Stroh"del

Serves: 12

1½ **pounds ground sausage**

¼ **cup sliced green onions**

1 **package (8 ounces) cream cheese**

2-3 **dashes hot pepper sauce**

½ **teaspoon Worcestershire sauce**

⅛ **teaspoon pepper**

6 **sheets frozen phyllo dough, thawed**

¼ **cup margarine or butter, melted**

1 **cup plus 2 tablespoons unseasoned bread crumbs**

Preheat oven to 375 degrees. Brown sausage in a saucepan. Drain fat. Add green onions, cream cheese, hot pepper sauce, Worcestershire sauce, and pepper. Cook and stir until thoroughly combined. Set aside. Lightly brush one phyllo sheet with butter. Layer another phyllo sheet on top and brush with butter. Sprinkle with ½ cup bread crumbs. Repeat with 2 more phyllo sheets and another ½ cup bread crumbs. Top with remaining 2 phyllo sheets. Spread sausage mixture along long edge of phyllo, leaving 1-inch from short edges. Fold short edges in and roll up from long side. Place roll seam side down on a greased baking sheet. Brush with remaining butter. Sprinkle with 2 tablespoons bread crumbs. Bake 15-20 minutes or until golden browned. Slice and serve warm.

Our family loves this one! We playfully renamed it from Sausage Strudel to Sausage "Stroh"del. We serve it Christmas morning along with the Christmas Buffet recipe before opening our stockings. This recipe was printed in a story written about Mom in the January 1993 issue of Country America *magazine.*

Breakfast Quiche   Serves: 8

**8-10 slices bacon, cut into
       small pieces**
¼   cup chopped yellow onion
4   eggs
2   cups half-and-half
¼   teaspoon seasoned salt
¼   teaspoon pepper
½   teaspoon dried parsley
**1½   cups shredded Swiss
       cheese**
**1   (9-inch) pie crust,
       unbaked
       *(see Jeanette's Pie Dough
       recipe, page 200)***

Preheat oven to 350 degrees.
Fry bacon in a skillet until
browned but not crispy. With a
slotted spoon, remove bacon
and place in a small bowl lined
with a paper towel. Cook onions
slightly in drippings and drain.
Add onions to bacon. Beat eggs
in a bowl. Stir in half-and-half,
seasoned salt, pepper, and
parsley. Spoon bacon and onion
mixture over bottom of pie crust.
Sprinkle cheese over bacon and
onions. Pour egg mixture over
cheese. Bake 50 minutes or
until firm to the touch and
slightly golden browned.

*I love this quiche, especially with the Swiss cheese
that gives it a wonderful sharp flavor. This was one of
Mom's signature dishes that people ordered in advance
for the holidays.*

Christmas Buffet

Serves: 8

7	slices white bread
1	package (8 ounces) shredded Cheddar cheese
6	eggs
3	cups milk
½	teaspoon salt
¼	teaspoon pepper
1	teaspoon dry mustard
8	portion slices ham, ¼-inch thick

Preheat oven to 325 degrees. Break bread into small pieces onto the bottom of a 13x9x2-inch baking dish. Spread cheese on top of bread. Whisk together eggs, milk, salt, pepper, and mustard. Pour over bread and cheese. Bake for 30 minutes. Arrange ham on top. Bake for another 25 minutes or until the egg is firm to the touch and ham is hot.

Mom made this for us every Christmas. We would eat this with donuts, juice, and coffee and then run for the stockings. Mom sometimes would use 1 pound of ground sausage instead of the ham slices. She would cook the sausage, crumble it and mix it in with the bread and cheese. This recipe can be made the night before and then baked in the morning.

Fresh Fruit Parfait with Stroh Ranch Jam   Serves: 6

1   **container (8 ounces) lemon yogurt**

1   **container (8 ounces) frozen whipped topping, thawed**

3   **tablespoons Stroh Ranch Wild Blackberry Jam or Stroh Ranch Razzleberry Jam**

1   **pound grapes**

1   **basket strawberries, sliced**

2   **mangos, sliced into bite size pieces**

3   **kiwis, sliced into bite size pieces**

1   **basket raspberries or blueberries**

1   **cup granola**

Combine yogurt, whipped topping, and jam to make a layering sauce. Spoon some sauce into the bottom of 6 large parfait glasses. Layer the grapes, strawberries, mangos, and kiwis alternating with the sauce. Layer to the top of the glasses. Top the last fruit with sauce. Sprinkle raspberries or blueberries on top of sauce. Sprinkle granola on top and serve chilled.

This is a beautiful dessert to share with family and friends. We usually served it during the summer when fruit is at its peak. The jam can be found on our website at www.pjsgourmet.com.

75

Hot Spiced Cider

Serves: 8

8   cups apple cider
⅓   cup packed brown sugar
3   sticks cinnamon
1   teaspoon whole allspice
16   whole cloves
1   orange, thinly sliced

Combine apple cider and brown sugar in a large saucepan. Place cinnamon sticks, allspice and cloves in a double thickness of 100-percent-cotton cheesecloth. Bring up corners of cheesecloth and tie with a string. Add spice bag and orange slices to cider mixture. Bring to boil. Reduce heat. Cover and simmer for 10 minutes. With slotted spoon, remove orange slices and spice bag. Discard. Serve cider with additional orange slices, if desired.

This is a delicious holiday recipe that was printed in a story written about Mom in the January 1993 issue of Country America *magazine.*

76

Tom and Jerry-Style Eggnog

Serves: 32

Eggnog Mix

6   **egg yolks**
¾   **cup water**
6   **egg whites**
¼   **teaspoon cream of tartar**
2   **pounds sifted powdered sugar**

Each Serving

1   **cup very hot water**
1   **tablespoon brandy**
1   **tablespoon rum**
¼   **cup eggnog mix**
Ground nutmeg

Combine egg yolks and water in a medium saucepan. Cook and stir over medium heat about 6 minutes or until mixture is thickened and coats a metal spoon. Remove from heat. Cover with plastic wrap and let cool. Beat egg whites and cream of tartar until stiff peaks form. Set aside. Fold in cooled egg yolk mixture in egg whites. Gradually beat in half of powdered sugar. Beat in remaining powdered sugar. Cover. Freeze until serving time. Freeze any remaining mix. To serve, combine hot water, brandy, rum, and eggnog mix in a large mug. Sprinkle with nutmeg.

Note: For nonalcoholic servings, use 1 cup hot milk instead of water and ¼ teaspoon rum extract for the alcohol.

This is another one of Mom's great holiday recipes that was printed in a story written about her in the January 1993 issue of Country America *magazine.*

Country Sunrise

Serves: 10

½ **gallon peach or tropical fruit sherbet**

1 **bottle Muscat Canelli wine**

Sliced nectarines and mint sprigs for garnish

Blend sherbet and wine in a food processor. Pour into 6-ounce parfait glasses. Freeze for no longer than 30 minutes. Serve with a nectarine slice on the edge of the glass and a sprig of mint.

This was one of Pat Denny's recipes typed on Pat and Mom's letterhead when they first started Jeanette's Country Cooking. They first served it to a group of food editors in 1987. I prefer making this flavorful dessert with Barra of Mendocino Muscat Canelli. You can also serve it in fluted glasses. It does not need a spoon to enjoy as long as you keep it in the freezer for only 30 minutes.

78

Soups
&
Salads

CONTENTS

Crab Chowder   Serves: 12

8	bottles (8 ounces each) bottled clam juice
1	cup dry sherry
1	tablespoon minced garlic
12	parsley sprigs
4	bay leaves
4	potatoes, diced
6	slices bacon
2	small white onions, finely chopped
1 1/4	cups finely chopped celery
2	tablespoons chopped fresh thyme
1/2	cup all-purpose flour
3	cups half-and-half
1	teaspoon salt
1/2	teaspoon pepper
2	dashes hot pepper sauce
3/4	pound cooked crabmeat

Chopped parsley for garnish

In a 4-quart stockpot, bring clam juice, sherry, garlic, parsley sprigs, and bay leaves to boil. Reduce heat. Simmer, uncovered, 15 minutes. Strain mixture through a double layer of cheesecloth into a medium bowl. Set clam broth aside. Cook potatoes in a pot of salted boiling water until tender. Drain potatoes and immerse into cold water. Drain potatoes and set aside. In a large sauté pan, cook bacon until crisp. Crumble and set aside. Reserve bacon drippings and pan. Add onions and celery to bacon drippings and sauté until tender. Stir in thyme and flour. Gradually whisk in clam broth. Bring to boil. Transfer mixture to stockpot and simmer for 15 minutes. Stir in half-and-half, salt, pepper, hot pepper sauce, potatoes, and bacon. Add crabmeat to stockpot before serving and heat thoroughly. Ladle chowder into bowls and garnish with parsley.

We enjoyed testing this recipe. I used canned crabmeat that I found in the fish market of our local grocery store. This recipe is rich, creamy, and flavorful!

81

Crab Cioppino

Serves: 6

Soup

½ cup olive oil

½ cup butter

2 yellow onions, finely chopped

6 garlic cloves, finely chopped

2 cups finely chopped parsley

2 cups finely chopped celery

1 tablespoon dried rosemary

1 tablespoon finely chopped sage

½ teaspoon dried thyme

½ teaspoon ground allspice

1 tablespoon salt

½ teaspoon pepper

2 hot chile peppers, seeded and chopped

½ bottle (5 ounces bottle) hot pepper sauce

1 bottle (14 ounces) ketchup

1 bottle (12 ounces) cocktail sauce

2 cans (15 ounces each) tomato sauce

4 cans water

2 bay leaves

½ cup bourbon

Seafood

3 cooked crabs, cleaned, halved and cracked

2 pounds medium shrimp, shelled

1 pound clams, live left overnight in water to purge out the grit

1 pound scallops

1 pound cod

Combine oil, butter, onions, garlic, parsley, celery, rosemary, sage, thyme, allspice, salt, pepper, chilies, hot pepper sauce, ketchup, cocktail sauce, tomato sauce, water, bay leaves, and bourbon in a large stockpot. Bring to boil. Reduce heat and simmer for 5 hours. It is best to do this the day before serving. About 15 minutes before serving, add crab, shrimp, clams, scallops, and fish. Remove bay leaves. Serve in large bowls with French bread and salad.

Sweet Corn and Shrimp Soup   Serves: 8

2   carrots, sliced
2   onions, chopped
2   leeks, chopped, white part only
2   ears corn, shucked and kernels cut off of cob
⅓   cup peanut oil
2   tablespoons minced ginger
½   bunch cilantro leaves, chopped
½   bunch basil leaves, chopped
1   can (13.5 ounces) sweetened coconut milk
½   cup heavy cream
7 ½ cups chicken broth
½   cup cornstarch
½   cup chicken broth
2   pounds medium shrimp
2   limes, juiced
Salt and pepper to taste

Sauté carrots, onions, leeks, and corn in oil until tender. Transfer vegetables to a large stockpot. Add ginger, cilantro, basil, coconut milk, and cream. Add 7 ½ cups broth. Simmer until thoroughly heated. In a small bowl, combine cornstarch with broth. Mix until creamy. Whisk cornstarch mixture into soup. Cook and stir about 10 minutes until thickened. Remove shells and tails from shrimp. Add shrimp and lime juice to soup. Simmer for 10 minutes. Serve hot.

This is a Thai styled soup that our tasters loved. You may even want to add some chopped red chilies to make it spicier.

83

Artichoke Bisque   Serves: 6

2	tablespoons butter
1	yellow onion, chopped
4	tablespoons all-purpose flour
6	cups chicken broth
3	packages (8 ounces each) frozen artichoke hearts, thawed
1	cup half-and-half

Salt and pepper to taste

Minced fresh parsley for garnish

Melt butter in a 4-quart saucepan. Sauté onions about 10 minutes until golden browned. Stir in flour to coat onions. Add broth and artichoke hearts. Bring to boil. Reduce heat and simmer about 15 minutes or until thickened. In a blender, purée mixture in batches until smooth. Return to saucepan. Stir over low heat and add half-and-half. Add salt and pepper and heat thoroughly. You may want to add more half-and-half to taste. Ladle hot bisque into bowls and garnish with parsley.

Mom and I had fun with this recipe. We tried it with many other vegetables in place of the artichokes. We enjoyed it with green beans, or asparagus (strained well because of the fibers) or you could even try it with squash. I usually serve it before the main course in small soup cups with garlic French bread or with our Coffee Can Bread recipe.

Butternut Squash and Leek Soup

Serves: 10

2   **tablespoons butter**

2   **medium leeks, sliced, white part only**

4   **garlic cloves, minced**

½   **teaspoon dried thyme**

½   **cup white wine**

2   **medium butternut squashes**

5   **cups chicken broth**

Salt and black or white pepper to taste

¼   **pound Gruyère cheese, grated**

1   **small bunch fresh thyme, leaves only and chopped**

Melt butter in a stockpot. Add leeks, garlic, and thyme. Cook until leeks are tender. Add wine and simmer for 5 minutes. Peel, seed and cut squash into small cubes, approximately 4 cups. Add cubed squash and broth. Cook over medium heat until squash is a smooth consistency. Purée soup in a blender and return to stockpot. Thin soup with more broth if necessary to desired consistency. Add salt and pepper. Ladle soup into bowls. Sprinkle with cheese and thyme.

Note: To make the squash easier to handle, try cutting the squash in half and remove the seeds. Cut each half into 4 pieces and microwave until you can insert a knife somewhat easily, then scoop the flesh out of the rind. This can be faster, but soup texture is better if you follow original method.

Thelma and Bob Levy of the Supper Club shared this savory soup for the cookbook in honor of Mom. Everyone loved tasting it and enjoyed the added flavor of the cheese and thyme sprinkled on top.

85

Corn and Wild Rice Soup with Smoked Sausage

Serves: 12

5   cups chicken broth

1¼ cups wild rice

3¾ cups frozen whole kernel corn, thawed

1½ cups chicken broth

16   ounces fully cooked smoked sausage, cut into ½-inch cubes

2   tablespoons olive oil

3   carrots, peeled and diced

2   medium onions, chopped

6   cups chicken broth

2½ cups frozen whole kernel corn, thawed

1½ cups half-and-half

Salt and pepper to taste

Bring broth to boil. Add wild rice and simmer about 50 minutes or until all liquid is absorbed. Set aside. In a food processor, purée corn and chicken broth. Set aside. Sauté sausage in oil. Add carrots and onions and sauté until tender. In a large stockpot, combine chicken broth, sausage and vegetables. Simmer for 15 minutes. Add cooked rice, puréed corn, and whole corn. Simmer for 15 minutes. Stir in half-and-half, salt, and pepper. Serve hot. Soup may be made 2 days in advance.

Dad loved this recipe and called it a "keeper." It's a hearty soup that tastes even better the next day.

Kale and Bean Soup
Serves: 8

1 tablespoon olive oil

8 large garlic cloves, chopped

1 medium yellow onion, chopped

4 cups chopped kale

4 cups chicken or vegetable broth

2 cans (15 ounces each) white kidney beans

4 plum tomatoes, chopped

2 teaspoons dried Italian herb seasoning

1 teaspoon salt

½ teaspoon pepper

1 cup half-and-half

Chopped parsley for garnish

Heat oil in a large stockpot. Sauté garlic and onions until soft. Add kale and sauté, stirring, until wilted. Add broth, beans, tomatoes, herb seasoning, salt, and pepper. Using a blender, purée soup in batches until creamy. Return soup to stockpot. Simmer for 15 minutes. Add half-and-half and heat thoroughly before serving. Ladle into soup bowls and sprinkle with parsley.

My mom always used kale for lining baskets of fresh vegetables. Kale is a deep green color with frilly leaves and is perfect for decoratively lining plates and baskets. After enjoying this recipe I now know it tastes good too! Kale is usually available year-round and is rich in vitamins A and C, folic acid, calcium, and iron.

87

Lentil Soup

Serves: 12

1½ cups dried French green lentils, soaked overnight
5 slices bacon, finely chopped
1 cup chopped yellow onion
2 cups chopped celery
1 cup diced carrots
½ garlic clove, finely chopped
2 cups peeled, and diced baking potatoes
1 can (6 ounces) tomato paste
2 whole cloves
2 bay leaves
1 teaspoon ground cumin
5 cups cold water
4 cups beef broth
1 tablespoon salt
⅛ teaspoon pepper
2 tablespoons red wine vinegar
2 cups cubed ham or sliced sausage
1 cup thinly sliced leeks

Cover lentils with water and soak overnight. In a 6-quart stockpot, sauté bacon until cooked through but not crispy. Add onions, celery, carrots, and garlic. Cook for 5 minutes over medium heat. Drain lentils. Add lentils, potatoes, tomato paste, cloves, bay leaves, cumin, water, broth, salt, and pepper. Cover and simmer for about 1 hour, 30 minutes or until lentils are tender. Add vinegar, ham, and leeks. Keep warm until ready to serve.

Our close family friends, Thelma and Bob Levy of the Supper Club, shared this delicious recipe for the cookbook in honor of Mom. It reminds me of the lentil soup my mom made after every Easter. Mom enjoyed making soups and used any leftover ham for either lentil soup or pea soup. I did not find my mom's lentil soup recipe so I am thankful to the Levy's for sharing their special recipe.

SOUPS & SALADS

Onion Soup

4 large yellow onions, thinly sliced
1 tablespoon butter
1 tablespoon vegetable oil
1/4 teaspoon sugar
2 tablespoons all-purpose flour
6 cups chicken broth
1/4 cup dry white wine
Salt and pepper to taste
4 slices sourdough bread, cut 1/2-inch thick
2 teaspoons olive oil
1 garlic clove, halved
2 tablespoons brandy
1 cup grated Swiss cheese

In a covered 4-quart saucepan, cook onions slowly with butter and oil for 15 minutes, stirring occasionally. Add sugar. Increase to moderate heat and sauté onions, stirring frequently, about 20 minutes or until golden browned. Stir in flour and cook another 2 minutes. Add broth, white wine, salt, and pepper. Cover and simmer for 1 hour. Toast bread slices at 350 degrees oven for 15 minutes. Brush each slice with 1/2 teaspoon oil and rub with garlic. Toast bread another 15 minutes or until lightly browned. Add brandy to hot soup just before serving. Divide soup into large ovenproof bowls. Sprinkle 1/2 cup of the cheese evenly into the four bowls. Place bread on top of the soup. Sprinkle remaining cheese over the bread. Broil until cheese is golden browned. Serve hot.

This is a great soup. The brandy really adds to the flavor! Depending on the size of the bowls, you might want to add two slices of bread to each bowl to cover more of the soup. I also prefer using chicken broth instead of beef broth.

89

Pumpkin Potato Soup

Serves: 9

2	tablespoons butter
2	tablespoons olive oil
1	yellow onion, chopped
2	celery ribs, sliced
2	leeks, sliced, white part only
5	large garlic cloves, minced
1	tablespoon firmly packed brown sugar
2	tablespoons minced fresh thyme leaves
1	tablespoon minced fresh sage leaves
1	large bay leaf
1	pound thin-skinned white potatoes, scrubbed and cut into 1-inch cubes
1/2	teaspoon ground nutmeg
1	teaspoon salt
1/2	teaspoon freshly ground white pepper
3	cups chicken broth
3	cans (15 ounces each) pumpkin
1	cup chicken broth
2/3	cup half-and-half

Minced fresh chives and/or parsley for garnish

In a large, nonstick stockpot, melt butter with oil over medium-low heat. Add onions, celery, leeks, and garlic. Cover and cook for 5 minutes until onions are soft. Increase heat slightly and stir in brown sugar, thyme, sage, and bay leaf. Cook, stirring, for 1 minute. Add potatoes, nutmeg, salt, pepper, and 3 cups broth. Bring to boil. Reduce heat, cover and cook for 20 minutes or until potatoes are soft. Discard bay leaf. Purée soup and pumpkin in batches in a blender. Return puréed soup to a large, clean stockpot. Stir in 1 cup broth and half-and-half. Mix well and heat without boiling. Taste and adjust seasonings. Thin with more broth and/or half-and-half as desired. Ladle soup into heated bowls and garnish with chives or parsley.

This is my favorite soup! I love the flavor and richness of this soup and can't wait to eat it for lunch the next couple of days.

90

SOUPS & SALADS

Hearty Meatball Soup

Serves: 8

1   large yellow onion, chopped
2   stalks celery, chopped
2   carrots, sliced in half lengthwise and sliced
2   garlic cloves, minced
2   tablespoons olive oil
3   cans (14 ounces each) beef broth
1   quart water
1   small cabbage, quartered, cored and sliced on diagonal 1/4-inch thick
2   medium white potatoes, peeled and cubed
1   can (16 ounces) Italian style diced tomatoes
1   teaspoon dried basil
1   teaspoon dried oregano
1/4   teaspoon pepper
1   teaspoon salt
1   cup red wine
1/4   cup red wine vinegar

1   can (15 ounces) white beans, drained
1 1/2   cups angel hair pasta, broken into 1-inch pieces
1   package (2 pounds) frozen Italian turkey meatballs, thawed
Parmesan cheese

Sauté onions, celery, carrots, and garlic in olive oil until onions are tender. Set aside. In a large stockpot, bring broth and water to boil. Add cabbage, potatoes, tomatoes, basil, oregano, pepper, salt, red wine, and vinegar. Cover and simmer 45 minutes. Add white beans, onion mixture, and pasta. Cook for 15 minutes, stirring occasionally. Add meatballs and simmer for 15 minutes. Ladle soup in bowls and sprinkle with Parmesan cheese.

Our close family friends, Carole and Roy Stokes, shared this delicious recipe in honor of Mom. Roy and Carole have known my parents a long time. They all went to school together in Burlingame, CA. Mom always considered Carole an amazing cook, and I know Mom would have loved this recipe!

91

Vegetable and Beef Soup

Serves: 6

1½ **pounds beef stew meat, cubed**
2 **tablespoons butter**
1 **yellow onion, chopped**
1 **can (14.5 ounces) diced tomatoes with juice**
1 **can (15 ounces) mixed vegetables, drained**
2 **teaspoons salt**
¼ **teaspoon pepper**
1 **can (6 ounces) vegetable juice**
¼ **teaspoon chili powder**
½ **teaspoon garlic salt**
1 **tablespoon Worcestershire sauce**
8 **cups water**

Brown meat in butter in a large sauté pan. Add onions and sauté about 10 minutes. In a large stockpot, combine meat, onions, tomatoes, mixed vegetables, salt, pepper, vegetable juice, chili powder, garlic salt, Worcestershire sauce, and water. Simmer for 2 hours and serve hot with your favorite bread.

The can of mixed vegetables made this recipe easy. The vegetable juice adds great flavor to this wonderful soup.

Country-Style Turkey Salad

Yields: 4½ cups

1 pound roasted or smoked turkey, finely chopped

1 cup minced green onions

1 cup chopped romaine lettuce

1 cup mayonnaise

Combine turkey, green onions, lettuce, and mayonnaise. Refrigerate until chilled. Spoon salad into sliced cream puffs *(see Cream Puff recipe on page 27)* or use inside your favorite bread.

I tested the recipe with smoked turkey and everyone loved it. I made the cream puffs and filled them with the turkey salad to serve as an appetizer. Mom's favorite way to serve it was inside of cream puffs or croissants. We also enjoyed spooning some over romaine lettuce leaves.

93

Black Bean Salad

Serves: 8

2	large tomatoes, seeded and diced
½	red onion, minced
½	cup chopped fresh cilantro leaves
1	can (16 ounces) black beans, rinsed and drained
1	can (15.25 ounces) whole kernel sweet corn, drained
1	can (14.5 ounces) hearts of palm, drained, cut into ¼-inch rounds
¼	cup olive oil
3	tablespoons fresh lime juice
1	teaspoon ground coriander

Salt and pepper to taste

Combine tomatoes, onions, cilantro, beans, corn, hearts of palm, oil, juice, coriander, salt, and pepper. Refrigerate. Serve chilled as a side dish.

Note: This recipe can be made a day ahead to allow the beans and vegetables to marinate longer.

Our wonderful friends and neighbors, Marty and Nancy Smith, shared this great recipe in honor of Mom. They made it for us one day, and our family loved it. It would pair perfectly with a barbecued tri-tip (with Stroh Ranch Marinade of course)! I am so thankful to Marty and Nancy for being my lead tasters. They took the job very seriously, and I can tell they loved every minute.

Marinated Mushroom Salad

Serves: 6

1	cup vegetable oil
2	teaspoons salt
¼	cup chopped fresh basil
2½	teaspoons Dijon mustard
½	teaspoon pepper
½	teaspoon paprika
5	tablespoons white wine vinegar or golden balsamic vinegar
4	teaspoons lemon juice
2	pounds sliced mushrooms
1½	cups thinly sliced green onions
½	pint small cherry tomatoes

In a large bowl, combine oil, salt, basil, mustard, pepper, paprika, vinegar, and lemon juice. Beat until well blended. Add mushrooms and green onions. Marinate for 1 hour at room temperature, stirring occasionally. Just before serving, add some cherry and/or pear tomatoes for color. Toss and serve.

Supper Club members John and Karen Moon shared this recipe in honor of Mom. Karen told me this is truly one of her favorite salads to serve to her friends. She loves to serve it all year long! The cherry and pear tomatoes add so much color to her salad. She suggests finding any kind of small fresh tomatoes during the off season. I also tested it with golden balsamic vinegar, and that tasted great too!

95

California Broccoli Salad

Serves: 6

Dressing

1	**cup mayonnaise**
½	**cup sugar**
3	**tablespoons cider vinegar**
¼	**teaspoon pepper**

Salad

2	**large heads broccoli, cut into florets**
½	**small red onion, thinly sliced**
1	**cup raisins**
12	**ounces water chestnuts, chopped**
1	**cup sunflower seeds (optional)**
8	**slices (or more) bacon, cut into ¼-inch pieces, cooked and drained**

Blend mayonnaise, sugar, vinegar, and pepper until smooth. Blanch broccoli 1-2 minutes until bright green and still crisp-tender. Cool. Combine broccoli, onions, raisins, water chestnuts, and sunflower seeds in a large glass bowl. Add dressing and gently toss to coat. Sprinkle with bacon. Refrigerate at least 2-4 hours.

I enjoyed testing this salad especially with the water chestnuts in it. Mom loved broccoli. In fact she loved all vegetables. I'm not a big broccoli lover but had two helpings the night I tested it! It tasted fine without the sunflower seeds. If you want to have some nuts in it, other options could be chopped walnuts or pecans.

Spinach Salad

Serves: 8

2	large bunches fresh spinach, stemmed
2	tablespoons white wine vinegar
1	tablespoon white vermouth
2	teaspoons Dijon mustard
1	teaspoon soy sauce
1/2	teaspoon curry powder
1/2	teaspoon sugar
1/2	teaspoon salt
1/4	teaspoon pepper
1/3	cup vegetable oil
1	green apple, peeled, cored and chopped
1/3	cup peanuts
1/4	cup golden raisins
3	green onions, minced

Place spinach in a large salad bowl. In a small bowl, blend together vinegar, vermouth, mustard, soy sauce, curry, sugar, salt, pepper, and oil. Sprinkle apples, peanuts, raisins, and green onions over spinach. Pour dressing over salad and serve chilled.

We love the dressing. The sweet apple and raisins mixed with the salty peanuts and delicious dressing is a wonderful mix of flavors. After testing it, my dad was ready to serve it to the Supper Club he belongs to!

97

Potato Salad

Serves: 6

2 pounds red potatoes
1 ¼ cups real mayonnaise
2 hard-cooked eggs, chopped
¼ teaspoon garlic salt
½ teaspoon pepper
½ teaspoon seasoned salt
1 teaspoon dried parsley
3 tablespoons chopped red onion (optional)

Wash potatoes and cut out the small stem. Place potatoes in a stockpot of hot tap water. The potatoes should be just covered with water. Bring to boil. Cook for 25 minutes or until a fork easily passes half way into a potato. Drain and let cool completely. Chop potatoes into small pieces. Combine potatoes, mayonnaise, eggs, garlic salt, pepper, seasoned salt, parsley, and red onions. Mix well. Refrigerate until ready to serve.

This is the potato salad Mom served on many of her catering jobs. She also supplied the deli at Diamond Jim's and the deli at Forks Ranch Market in Ukiah with this potato salad every Monday. Mom originally used brown potatoes, but changed to red potatoes because they were easier to prepare. Our family actually preferred the red as the years went by. Mom later added red onions to the red potatoes. For those of you who enjoyed the deli salads, they always had chopped red onions in them. We prefer to use real mayonnaise. Mom always made the seasonings salty and added extra mayonnaise because the salt would back off and the mayonnaise would soak in after a day or two. If you serve the salad the night you prepare it, the seasonings will be fine.

Raspberry Vinegar Poppy Seed Dressing

Yields: 1½ cups

Dressing

¼ **cup sugar**
1 **teaspoon salt**
2 **tablespoons minced green onions**
1 **cup peanut oil**
2 **teaspoons dry mustard**
⅔ **cup raspberry vinegar**
2 **tablespoons poppy seeds**

Salad

Mesclun salad greens
Goat cheese or blue cheese, crumbled
Slivered almonds, toasted

Combine sugar, salt, green onions, oil, mustard, vinegar, and poppy seeds in a bowl. Place mesclun in a salad bowl. Drizzle dressing over top. Toss to coat. Top with cheese and almonds. Refrigerate. Serve chilled.

This recipe came from our friend Pat Nicholson, a member of the Supper Club, who shared it in honor of Mom. She told us she has perfected it over the years, and I agree. I love the sweet mixed with the tang of the vinegar. I served it over mesclun mix, but it would also be great over romaine lettuce. Mom served a dressing very similar to this one over the years, but she wanted me to keep it a secret in case we want to release it through PJ's Gourmet, my specialty food business.

99

Jeanette's Caesar Dressing

Serves: 10

1 **bottle Girard's Caesar Dressing**
2 **tablespoons dry Caesar dressing**
²/₃ **cup vegetable oil**
¹/₄ **cup grated Parmesan cheese**
2 **garlic cloves, minced**
1 **teaspoon Worcestershire sauce**
¹/₈ **teaspoon pepper**
Large dash hot pepper sauce

Pour Girard's Caesar Dressing into a bowl. Put a little water into the bottle and shake well. Pour into the bowl. Add dry dressing, oil, Parmesan cheese, garlic, Worcestershire sauce, pepper, and hot pepper sauce and mix well. Serve with croutons on romaine lettuce.

Mom's customers really loved this recipe. On a typical day, she would multiply this recipe by 12! Traditional Caesar dressings were time consuming for her to make for hundreds of people, so she came up with this recipe with lots of help from our family friends, Tom and Linda Wakeman.

Maple Mustard Vinaigrette Dressing Yields: 2 cups

Dressing

⅓ **cup cider vinegar**
3 **garlic cloves**
2 **shallots, peeled**
1 **teaspoon ground pepper**
1 **tablespoon grainy mustard**
⅔ **cup maple syrup**
1 **cup canola oil**

Salad

Hearts of Romaine
Apples, chopped
Honey roasted almonds
Blue cheese, crumbled

Combine vinegar, garlic, shallots, pepper, mustard, and maple syrup in a food processor. Blend on high. Slowly add oil. Mix together romaine and apples. Sprinkle almonds and blue cheese on top. Serve with maple mustard vinaigrette dressing.

Howard and Peggy Howard, long-time family friends, shared this wonderful recipe with Mom. It made its debut at one of Peggy and Howard's great summer parties several years ago. I remember Mom getting so excited about it and asking for the recipe that night.

101

Sugared Nuts

Serves: 6

1½ **cups walnut halves**
⅛   **teaspoon salt**
1   **cup sugar**
½   **teaspoon cinnamon**
⅛   **teaspoon cream of tartar**
½   **teaspoon vanilla**
¼   **cup water**

Preheat oven to 350 degrees. Combine walnuts, salt, sugar, cinnamon, and cream of tartar. Add vanilla and water. Mix well. Pour mixture onto the middle of a baking sheet. Bake for 15 minutes, turning mixture over with a spatula every few minutes. Most of the water will evaporate off so you have a thick mixture. Transfer nuts from baking sheet to wax paper. Spread out nuts to keep from sticking to each other. Serve at room temperature.

This is an old recipe from our close friend, Kay Whittaker. My mom used this recipe over the last 40 years for topping a salad or eating as a snack. When I tested the recipe, John and I enjoyed them for dessert. My favorite use is adding it to the Maple Mustard Vinaigrette Dressing recipe. I make the romaine salad with apples and blue cheese and sprinkle the sugared nuts over the top. It is fabulous!

102

Red Hot Candy Salad

Serves: 8

1 package (6 ounces) cherry flavored gelatin

2 cups hot water

½ cup red cinnamon candy

1 cup hot water

½ cup chopped walnuts

1 cup chopped apples

In a small bowl, dissolve gelatin in hot water. In a small saucepan, combine candy and water. Cook and stir until candy dissolves. When dissolved, add enough water to make 2 cups of liquid. Add candy mixture to gelatin. Mix well. Pour mixture into an 8x8x2-inch glass dish. Cool in refrigerator until partially set. Mix in walnuts and apples. Return to refrigerator until set.

This is my favorite gelatin salad! Every year for my birthday Mom would grant me a dinner menu of my choice. This is the recipe I consistently asked for every year. Mom sometimes would cover it with whipped topping.

103

Holiday Gelatin Salad   Serves: 12

1   package (6 ounces) lime
    flavored gelatin
1   can (20 ounces) crushed
    pineapple with juice
1   package (8 ounces) cream
    cheese, softened
1   package (10.5 ounces)
    miniature marshmallows
2   cups hot water
1   cup mayonnaise
1   package (6 ounces)
    strawberry flavored gelatin
2   cups hot water
2   cups cold water

Combine lime gelatin, pineapple, cream cheese, marshmallows, water, and mayonnaise in a large saucepan. Cook over low heat, stirring constantly, until marshmallows and cream cheese melts. Pour mixture into a 13x9x2-inch baking dish. Refrigerate until set. Combine strawberry gelatin and water according to package directions. Cool slightly. Pour over lime gelatin. Refrigerate for 3 hours.

What a beautiful and delicious recipe this is! This is our holiday favorite and is served every Christmas. All of the gelatin salads in this cookbook are family favorites.

104

Cranberry Cream Salad   Serves: 8

1	**package (3 ounces) cherry flavored gelatin**
1	**cup hot water**
1	**can (16 ounces) whole cranberry sauce**
1/2	**cup finely diced celery**
1/4	**cup chopped walnuts**
1	**cup sour cream**

In a small bowl, dissolve gelatin in hot water. Refrigerate until slightly thickened. Break up cranberry sauce with a fork. Stir cranberry sauce, celery, and walnuts into gelatin. Fold in sour cream. Pour mixture into a 4-cup mold. Refrigerate until set.

I found this recipe in the Potter Valley Methodist Church cookbook. Mom had submitted it to the cookbook in 1983. She noted this salad is great with a turkey dinner and pretty at Christmas. I had long forgotten about this great recipe. It brought back wonderful memories when I tested it.

105

Orange Gelatin Salad

Serves: 12

2 packages (6 ounces each) orange flavored gelatin

4 cups orange juice

4 cups buttermilk

Combine gelatin and orange juice in a saucepan. Bring to boil. Remove from heat. Stir in buttermilk. Pour mixture into a 13x9x2-inch baking dish. Refrigerate until set.

My Grandma Nancy McRoberts made this gelatin salad every time we went to visit her. She would serve it over lettuce or just by itself. You can substitute other gelatin flavors for orange gelatin.

106

Entrées

CONTENTS

ENTRÉES

Prime Rib

Serves: 15

10 pounds rock salt
13 pound boneless prime rib
1 cup Worcestershire sauce
1 garlic bulb, peeled and chopped
20 egg whites, stiffly beaten
Au Jus and horseradish for garnish

Preheat oven to 350 degrees. Line an 18x12x4-inch baking pan with foil. Pour 1 inch of rock salt evenly onto the bottom of the pan. Place prime rib on top of rock salt. Pour Worcestershire sauce over entire prime rib. Sprinkle garlic evenly over prime rib. Build rock salt up halfway along the sides of prime rib. Spread egg whites evenly over entire prime rib, covering meat. Do not let any meat show. Bake for 2 hours, 30 minutes–3 hours or until internal temperature reaches 140 degrees. Cook less for rare meat. Let stand for 10 minutes before serving. Scrape egg white crust off the top of the meat. Lift up one side of the roast and scrape off the rock salt from the bottom and sides of the roast. Transfer to a platter and cut into 15-17 slices at the dinner table. Serve warm with au jus and horseradish.

Use this recipe for a large dinner gathering. This is a very unique way to cook a prime rib! The salt on the bottom permeates into the meat to give it added flavor while the egg whites seal in the juices during the cooking process. We all love this way of cooking a prime rib. It was a treat to pick off the loose, tender chunks on the bottom of the roast. Mom always used boneless prime ribs. I checked with our local stores and you can buy them in various sizes.

Ken and Jeanette's BBQ Tri-Tip

Serves: 4

2 pounds tri-tip beef roast, or a thick cut of top sirloin

⅓ bottle (12.7 ounces) Stroh Ranch Original Marinade

Place roast and marinade in a zip-top plastic bag. Refrigerate overnight, turning bag occasionally until ready to barbecue. Reserve excess marinade. Barbecue roast over medium coals (I prefer mesquite) or on medium on a gas grill for 30-40 minutes. Baste roast with reserved marinade to capture the delicious flavors. Cut across the grain and serve immediately.

This is the recipe that made Stroh Ranch Original Marinade (see www.pjsgourmet.com) famous. Jeanette's Country Cooking was known for the excellent tri-tips that my dad and Raul Gonzalez barbecued. It is important to baste the meat as it is being barbecued. Mom would traditionally serve it with her Caesar Salad, Red Potatoes with Bacon and Buttermilk Dressing and assorted dinner rolls. During the summer, she would add a fresh fruit salad.

Beef Burgundy

Serves: 6 large portions

2/3	cup all-purpose flour
1	tablespoon salt
1	teaspoon pepper
4	pounds beef, cut in 1-inch cubes
2	tablespoons butter
1	tablespoon vegetable oil
2	beef bouillon cubes
1	cup boiling water
2	cups burgundy wine
3/4	teaspoon dried thyme
1	bay leaf
1	garlic clove, crushed
4	large carrots, cut lengthwise
1	onion, sliced
1	pound mushrooms, sliced
2	tablespoons minced parsley for garnish

Preheat oven to 325 degrees. Combine flour, salt, and pepper in a bowl. Roll beef cubes in the seasoned flour reserving any leftover flour. Heat butter and oil in a large oven-proof skillet. Lightly brown meat one-third at a time. Pour off drippings and sprinkle reserved flour over meat. Dissolve bouillon cubes in boiling water. Add broth, wine, thyme, bay leaf, and garlic. Cover and cook in the oven for 45 minutes. Stir in carrots and onions. Continue cooking for 2 hours. Stir in mushrooms and cook an additional 15 minutes. Remove bay leaf. Serve in large soup bowls over your favorite pasta or rice. Garnish with parsley.

This is a flavorful and hearty meal. We use red wine from Mendocino County for the burgundy, usually a Cabernet, and pour more to go with the dinner.

111

Meatloaf with Smoky Jalapeño Honey Sauce   Serves: 6

2   **pounds ground beef**

1   **small yellow onion, chopped**

½   **cup Stroh Ranch Smoky Jalapeño Honey Sauce, Hot or Mild**

1½ **cups rolled old-fashioned oats**

½   **cup shredded Cheddar cheese**

½   **cup Parmesan cheese**

3   **eggs**

2   **tablespoons Worcestershire sauce**

1   **teaspoon garlic salt**

1   **teaspoon seasoned salt**

¾   **teaspoon salt**

Stroh Ranch Smoky Jalapeño Honey Sauce, Hot or Mild

Preheat oven to 350 degrees. Combine beef, onions, sauce, oats, Cheddar cheese, Parmesan cheese, eggs, Worcestershire sauce, garlic salt, seasoned salt, and salt in a large bowl. Knead until well combined. Shape mixture into a loaf. Place in a baking dish. Bake for 1 hour, 15 minutes. When finished baking, brush some Stroh Ranch Smoky Jalapeño Honey Sauce on top of the meatloaf. Return to the oven to heat the sauce on top. Serve hot.

I love Mom's meatloaf. I eat the leftover meatloaf for lunch the next day. I toast some bread, add the meatloaf and condiments and enjoy all over again.

112

Country Baked Ribs

Serves: 4

1 large rack baby back pork ribs or 4 pounds beef ribs

⅓ bottle (14.75 ounces) Stroh Ranch Smoky Jalapeño Honey Sauce, Hot or Mild

If possible, remove membrane off the back of the ribs. Boil ribs in a covered pot for 20 minutes. Drain. Arrange ribs on a baking sheet. Brush sauce on ribs. Bake at 350 degrees for 30 minutes or cook on the barbecue. Brush on more sauce as needed.

The Stroh Ranch Smoky Jalapeño Honey Sauces were released in 2001 (see www.pjsgourmet.com). This is one of our favorite ways to serve baby back ribs. The sauce is made with 40 percent honey, mustard and spices. It makes a beautiful glaze on all meats.

113

Viennese Pork Chops

Serves: 6

6 **boneless pork chops, 1-inch thick**

2 **tablespoons butter**

Salt and pepper to taste

4 **apples, peeled, cored and quartered**

12 **white pearl onions, ends cut and peeled**

¼ **cup raisins**

½ **cup sherry**

½ **cup water**

¼ **teaspoon ground nutmeg**

Dash of ground thyme

Preheat oven to 375 degrees. Brown pork chops in a skillet with butter about 5 minutes on each side. Pour off drippings. Sprinkle with salt and pepper. Arrange pork chops in a 13x9x2-inch baking dish. Cover with apples, onions, and raisins. In a small bowl, blend sherry, water, nutmeg and thyme. Pour mixture over pork chops. Cover and bake for 45 minutes. Uncover and bake an additional 15 minutes.

Grandma Stroh shared this delicious recipe with Mom. The pork chops are very tender. I enjoyed testing this recipe with a bite each of pork with a little pearl onion, apple and raisin.

Chicken Parmesan   Serves: 4

4   large boneless, skinless chicken breast halves
1   cup Italian seasoned bread crumbs
½   cup grated Parmesan cheese
2   tablespoons butter
1   tablespoon dry white wine
1   garlic clove, chopped
1   package (8 ounces) sliced mushrooms
1½ tablespoons olive oil
4   tablespoons butter
¼   cup dry white wine

Preheat oven to 350 degrees. Cook chicken in boiling water until turning white. Drain, rinse and set aside until cool. Combine bread crumbs and Parmesan cheese. Roll chicken in bread crumb mixture until completely covered and set aside. In a medium skillet, sauté butter, wine, and garlic for 5 minutes. Add mushrooms and sauté for another 5 minutes; set aside. Pour oil in the bottom of an 8x8x2-inch baking dish. Arrange chicken evenly onto the bottom of the dish. Spoon mushroom mixture in between and on the sides of chicken. Heat butter and wine in skillet until the butter has melted. Drizzle mixture over top of each chicken. Cover with foil. Bake for 40 minutes. Remove foil. Bake an additional 5 minutes. Serve hot.

I am thankful to our close family friend, Cathy Anello, for sharing this recipe in memory of Mom. Cathy worked for Mom as one of our event staff during the final years of Jeanette's Country Cooking. Cathy suggests serving it with your favorite pasta and a salad — and don't forget the wine!

115

Prosciutto Chicken Rolls
Serves: 8

8 **boneless, skinless chicken breast halves**

¼ **teaspoon pepper**

1 **package (8 ounces) cream cheese, softened**

¼ **cup fresh minced parsley**

1 **teaspoon minced garlic**

¼ **teaspoon salt**

8 **thin slices prosciutto**

⅔ **cup Italian seasoned bread crumbs**

½ **cup grated Parmesan cheese**

¼ **cup whole milk**

⅓ **cup butter, melted**

2 **tablespoons lemon juice**

⅛ **teaspoon paprika**

Preheat oven to 350 degrees. Roll or pound chicken between 2 sheets of wax paper and flatten to ¼-inch thickness using a rolling pin. Sprinkle chicken with pepper. In a bowl, combine cream cheese, parsley, garlic, and salt. Place one slice of prosciutto on each chicken. Spread cheese mixture evenly over prosciutto. May need to heat cheese mixture in the microwave for 20 seconds to make it easier to spread. In a separate bowl, combine bread crumbs and Parmesan cheese. Pour milk into another bowl. Roll up chicken starting at the short end. Dip each in milk. Roll into bread crumb mixture. Place seam side down in a lightly greased 13x9x2-inch baking dish. Combine butter and lemon juice in a bowl. Drizzle butter mixture over chicken and sprinkle with paprika. Bake 30-35 minutes or until lightly browned.

Our close family friends, Dennis Denny and Jette Vinding, shared this recipe in honor of Mom. They are members of the Supper Club that Mom and Dad had joined long ago. I love this chicken recipe and am so happy they shared it with us. I know for sure Mom would have loved this one and would have served it for catering jobs!

116

Baked Chicken with Sauce

Serves: 8

4 **pounds boneless, skinless chicken thighs**

2 **teaspoons seasoned salt**

1 **envelope (1.6 ounces) garlic and herb sauce mix**

1 **envelope (0.9 ounces) hollandaise sauce mix**

2½ cups milk

5 **tablespoons butter**

Fresh minced parsley for garnish

Preheat oven to 350 degrees. Arrange chicken on a baking sheet. Sprinkle evenly with seasoned salt. Bake 20 minutes or until cooked through. Transfer chicken to a 13x9x2-inch baking dish and set aside. Whisk two sauce mixes together with milk in a saucepan. Add butter and bring to boil, stirring frequently, until thickened. Drizzle sauce over chicken, covering all pieces. May not need all the sauce. Bake until thoroughly heated. Garnish with parsley and serve hot.

I would have named this differently, but this is what all of Mom's customers called this dish. It is a very simple recipe, but very tasty. It was one that was easy to make for 500 people! Mom always used chicken thighs, but you can also use chicken breasts.

117

Country Chicken Supreme

Serves: 8

Chicken

3	eggs, beaten
2	tablespoons milk
8	boneless, skinless chicken breast halves
1	cup all-purpose flour
1	cup bread crumbs
¼	cup butter
¼	cup oil

Sauce

1	can (14 ounces) chicken broth
¼	cup all-purpose flour
¼	cup butter
½	yellow onion, diced
½	teaspoon seasoned salt
¼	cup white wine

Preheat oven to 350 degrees. Whisk together eggs and milk in a shallow bowl. Dredge chicken in flour. Dip into egg mixture. Coat with breadcrumbs and place on a plate. Heat butter and oil in a large skillet. Quick fry chicken until golden browned on both sides. Reserve the pan. May need more oil and butter. Transfer chicken to a 13x9x2-inch baking dish. To make sauce, whisk together broth and flour in a small bowl. Melt butter in skillet and add broth mixture. Bring to boil and stir until thickened. Add onions, seasoned salt, and white wine and mix well. Pour sauce over chicken. Bake for 30 minutes.

I remember Mom serving this many times to our family. She would serve it with buttered pasta and a green salad. She had many great chicken dishes and this is definitely one of them!

118

Chicken Cacciatora

Serves: 4

4	**pound whole chicken, legs and thighs halved and breast quartered**
½	**cup olive oil**
3	**garlic cloves, pressed**
½	**cup all-purpose flour**
1½	**teaspoons salt**
¼	**teaspoon black pepper**
2	**eggs, beaten**
¼	**cup milk**
1	**cup grated Parmesan cheese**
3½	**cups tomatoes, chopped**
1¼	**teaspoons salt**
1	**teaspoon dried oregano**
½	**teaspoon pepper**
1	**teaspoon dried parsley**
1	**teaspoon dried basil**
1	**package (8 ounces) sliced fresh mushrooms**
1	**sweet bell pepper, chopped**
1	**cup red wine**
Hot cooked rice	

Remove skin on all chicken pieces. Heat oil and garlic in a large skillet. Combine flour, salt, and pepper in a bowl. Combine eggs and milk in a separate bowl. Pour the Parmesan cheese in a separate bowl. Dredge chicken in flour, dip in egg mixture and roll in Parmesan cheese. Cook chicken in skillet until golden browned on both sides. Drain extra oil. In a bowl, combine tomatoes, salt, oregano, pepper, parsley, basil, mushrooms, and peppers. Add tomato mixture to chicken. Pour in red wine and mix well. Cover and simmer about 20 minutes or until chicken is tender. Serve hot over rice.

I am so excited I found this recipe! It is delicious and beautiful over rice. I loved it when my Grandma Stroh made it. I luckily found it handwritten by Mom on two small pieces of paper stuffed in a crock in the kitchen. My dad and husband loved it and called it a "keeper." The Parmesan cheese really adds to this recipe. We also suggest using 3 pounds of boneless, skinless breasts and/or thighs in place of a whole chicken.

119

Chicken Chow Mein   Serves: 6

Marinade

½	teaspoon salt
1	teaspoon fresh minced ginger
1	teaspoon soy sauce
2	drops sesame oil
¼	teaspoon sugar
1	tablespoon cornstarch

Chicken

3	pounds boneless, skinless chicken breast halves, cut into small chunks
1	tablespoon olive oil

Vegetables

1	yellow onion, sliced
½	pound snow peas, trimmed
2	stalks celery, diagonally sliced
1	carrot, diagonally sliced
1	pound mushrooms, sliced
2	green onions, chopped
1	can (8 ounces) water chestnuts, drained and halved
2	cans (8 ounces each) bamboo shoots

Sauce

1	can (14 ounces) chicken broth
¼	teaspoon sugar
4	teaspoons cornstarch
3	tablespoons soy sauce
1	tablespoon oyster sauce

Combine salt, ginger, soy sauce, sesame oil, sugar, and cornstarch into a bowl. Add chicken and mix well. Refrigerate chicken for 2 hours. Heat olive oil in a very large sauté pan or wok. Cook chicken until cooked through. Transfer chicken to a bowl. Add onions to pan and sauté until limp. May need to add more olive oil. Add snow peas, celery, carrots, mushrooms, green onions, water chestnuts, and bamboo shoots. Cook about 20 minutes or until tender. Return chicken to pan. To make sauce, blend broth, sugar, cornstarch, soy sauce, and oyster sauce in a small bowl. Add sauce to pan and heat until gravy thickens. Serve hot over jasmine rice.

Ken and Jeanette's BBQ Chicken   Serves: 6

2 **whole chickens,**
   4 pounds each

½ **bottle (12.7 ounces) Stroh**
   Ranch Original Marinade

Rinse chicken and remove giblets. Cut chicken in half, lengthwise so that you have 4 sides each with a breast, thigh, wing, and leg. Cut backbone from the two sides that still have it attached. Discard backbones. Remove skin off four halves and discard. Place chicken in a large zip-top plastic bag. Pour marinade over chicken and seal the bag. Place bag flat in the refrigerator. Marinate for 4-6 hours, turning bag occasionally. Barbecue chicken on medium coals with the lid on for 20 minutes on each side or until cooked through. Cut chicken halves into 2 pieces each and serve warm.

The marinade (see www.pjsgourmet.com) tastes great with these half chickens. Mom always bought "splits" of chicken (half chickens) without the backbone to barbecue because it was easy to cook them and gave her customers a variety of pieces to enjoy. The splits cook evenly so you don't have to worry about cooking different small pieces on the barbecue.

Sweet and Sour Chicken

Serves: 4

²/₃ cup sugar

2 tablespoons cornstarch

1 tablespoon paprika

1 can (20 ounces) pineapple chunks, reserve juice

¼ cup soy sauce

¼ cup rice vinegar

1 bell pepper, sliced

1 onion, sliced

1 carrot, sliced

1 tablespoon olive oil

2 boneless, skinless chicken breast halves, cooked and sliced

Hot cooked rice

Combine sugar, cornstarch, and paprika in a bowl. Pour pineapple juice into a 2 cup measuring cup. Reserve pineapple chunks. Add enough water to make 2 cups of liquid. Pour pineapple juice into a saucepan and add soy sauce and rice vinegar. Whisk in sugar mixture. Bring to boil for 1 minute. Remove sauce from heat. Sauté peppers, onions, and carrots in oil in a skillet 5 to 10 minutes. Stir in chicken, pineapple, and sauce. Heat thoroughly. Serve hot over white rice.

The sauce is flavorful and does not look like the unnatural red sauces we sometimes see in restaurants. You may want to thicken the sauce more with cornstarch if you are serving it alone without rice. It is wonderful on jasmine rice!

122

ENTRÉES

Lemon Chicken

Serves: 6

Chicken

6	boneless, skinless chicken breast halves
¾	**cup all-purpose flour**
3	**eggs, beaten**
1¼	**cups Italian seasoned bread crumbs**
4	**tablespoons butter**

Lemon Sauce

½	**cup butter**
¾	**cup lemon juice**
1	**jar (4 ounces) capers**

Preheat oven to 350 degrees. Dredge chicken in flour. Dip in egg and coat with bread crumbs. Cook chicken in a large skillet in the butter until done and golden browned. Place chicken breasts in a small baking dish. For the sauce, combine butter, lemon juice, and capers in a saucepan. Heat until butter melts. Pour mixture evenly over chicken. Bake about 35 minutes or until chicken is thoroughly heated.

Mom served this recipe mostly over the winter months, and our customers loved it. I would suggest using Meyer lemons for the juice if you can find them, otherwise, the bottled lemon juice works just fine.

123

Chicken with Mushrooms

Serves: 4

1   **chicken (4 pounds) cut up or 2 pounds boneless, skinless chicken breast halves**

Salt, pepper, and paprika to taste

4   **tablespoons butter**

1   **package (8 ounces) frozen artichoke hearts, thawed**

1   **package (8 ounces) sliced mushrooms**

2   **green onions, chopped**

2   **tablespoons butter**

2   **tablespoons all-purpose flour**

²/₃   **cup chicken broth**

½   **cup sherry**

¼   **teaspoon dried rosemary**

Preheat oven to 375 degrees. Remove skin from chicken pieces. Sprinkle with salt, pepper and paprika. Brown chicken in a skillet in butter. Place chicken in a 13x9x2-inch baking dish. Top with artichoke hearts. Sauté mushrooms and green onions in butter. Pour mixture over chicken. Combine flour, broth, sherry, and rosemary in a saucepan. Cook and stir until smooth. Pour sauce over chicken. Bake for 30 minutes.

My Dad and my husband love this one — especially with the artichoke hearts! The original recipe calls for a chicken cut up, but we all think it might be good with 2 to 3 pounds of boneless, skinless chicken breast halves.

124

Chicken Divan   Serves: 8

1	**large bunch fresh broccoli**
2	**large boneless, skinless chicken breasts halves, cooked**
2	**cans (10¾ ounces each) cream of chicken soup**
1	**cup mayonnaise**
¼	**cup white wine**
2	**tablespoons lemon juice**
½	**teaspoon curry powder**
½	**cup unseasoned bread crumbs**
1	**tablespoon butter, melted**
½	**cup shredded sharp Cheddar cheese**

Preheat oven to 350 degrees. Cut away thick stalk of broccoli and reserve the tops. Cook broccoli tops for 5 minutes in boiling water and drain. Cut chicken into long strips. Set aside. Blend soup, mayonnaise, wine, lemon juice, and curry. Combine bread crumbs and butter. Arrange chicken in a 13x9x2-inch baking dish. Layer broccoli over chicken. Pour soup mixture evenly over broccoli. Sprinkle with cheese. Spoon bread crumb mixture over cheese. Bake for 30 minutes.

Our close family friend, Susan Westcott Moon, shared this recipe in honor of Mom. Mom and Dad have known her since their high school days. Susan shared a love of collecting insulators with Mom and had fun just laughing with her. This is a wonderful recipe with added flavor from the curry powder and wine. I suggest serving it with fettuccine or other large flat noodles.

125

Raul's Enchiladas

Serves: 8

4 **pound whole chicken without giblets**

2 **garlic cloves**

½ **yellow onion, sliced**

3 **Roma tomatoes**

1 **can (6 ounces) tomato paste**

½ **yellow onion**

3 **garlic cloves**

1 **bell pepper, sliced**

¼ **cup olive oil**

1 **teaspoon salt**

Pepper to taste

18 **corn tortillas (5½ inches each)**

Olive oil

1 **can (19 ounces) red enchilada sauce**

1 **cup shredded Cheddar cheese**

1 **cup Monterey Jack cheese**

Dried parsley for garnish

Boil chicken in water with garlic and onions about 30 minutes until tender and cooked through. Drain. When cooled, remove meat from bones. Chop meat and set aside. In a food processor, purée tomatoes, tomato paste, onions, and garlic. In a large skillet, sauté peppers and tomato mixture in oil for 5 minutes. Add salt and pepper. Stir in meat and cook until liquid is absorbed. Let cool. In a pan over low heat, cook tortillas in oil for 30 seconds on each side until flexible. Divide meat mixture evenly between tortillas and roll up. Place seam side down into two 13x9x2-inch baking dishes. Pour enchilada sauce evenly over tortillas and sprinkle with Cheddar cheese and Monterey Jack cheese. Sprinkle with parsley. Bake at 350 degrees 30 minutes or until thoroughly heated.

These are great! They are so flavorful and beautiful on a plate with red rice and salad.

ENTRÉES

Baked Salmon with Herbed Crumb Topping · Serves: 6

3   **pounds skinless salmon fillets, 6-8 portion pieces**

4   **tablespoons butter, melted**

½   **cup chopped fresh Italian parsley**

¼   **cup plus 2 tablespoons freshly grated Parmesan cheese**

1   **tablespoon dried thyme leaves, crumbled**

2   **teaspoons grated lemon peel**

½   **teaspoon salt**

4   **small garlic cloves**

2½   **cups unseasoned bread crumbs**

6   **tablespoons butter, melted**

Parsley Mayonnaise *(see page 130)*

Preheat oven to 350 degrees. Rinse and pat dry fillets. Butter a 13x9x2-inch baking dish with 2 tablespoons melted butter. Place fillets in the dish and brush with remaining 2 tablespoons butter. For the topping, blend parsley, Parmesan cheese, thyme, lemon peel, salt, and garlic in a food processor. Transfer mixture to a medium bowl. Stir in bread crumbs and butter. Press bread crumb mixture onto fillets. May not need all of this mixture depending on the size of the fillets. Bake about 30 minutes or until fish is opaque in center. Serve with Parsley Mayonnaise *(on page 130)*.

This is a fantastic dish that will amaze your guests. The Parsley Mayonnaise perfectly complements the herbed topping on the salmon. Mom loved serving great salmon recipes and this is one that is definitely memorable.

127

John Moon and Jeanette's Cedar Plank Salmon

Serves: 6

Cedar plank, 18x6x2-inches
¼ cup unsalted butter
5 garlic cloves, crushed
3 pounds wild salmon fillet, with skin
1 lemon
Kale (optional)
Lemon curls (optional)

Soak the cedar plank in water for an hour so it will smolder rather than burn on the grill. Melt butter in a small saucepan. Add garlic and sauté about 5 minutes until softened. Place fillet on a platter. Drizzle butter and garlic mixture over salmon. Squeeze lemon juice over salmon. Set aside. Salmon is cooked using the indirect method. If using charcoal briquettes, start them on one side of your barbecue. When briquettes have white ash on them, place the cedar plank on the grill so that only the outside edges of the planks are exposed to direct heat. For a gas grill, follow the manufacturer's directions for indirect cooking. Transfer fillet skin side down onto the plank. Place on barbecue. Cover grill with lid and cook for 30-35 minutes. The fillet is cooked when internal temperature reaches 135 degrees (measured between the flakes). Remove fillet from the plank using two spatulas to minimize it breaking apart. Place the spatulas between the meat and the skin and slide forward to remove the skin. Place fillet on a platter and serve warm. For an added presentation, line the edges of the platter with fresh kale. Place salmon in the middle. Slice a lemon into thin circles. Cut the flesh from the rind and make one cut through the rind to make long pieces. Twist rind into curls and decorate the platter.

I am so thankful to John Moon, our close family friend, for writing this down for me. Mom put this recipe together, and John was the chef at his house 10 years ago when he and Karen had a Supper Club dinner. It was a hit! John suggests finding a cedar plank suitable for your barbecue. He prefers a thicker plank 1 ½ to 2-inches because it lasts longer and creates more flavor. He has a charcoal Weber and uses two 18-inch planks placed side by side which allows him to cook two fillets at one time. He shared this tidbit with me, "In the more affluent areas the planks may be soaked in Pinot Noir to increase flavor. We find water works just fine where we live." He also mentioned "the smell coming from the top vent as you are cooking will serve as an attractant for your guests to hover around the cooking area. Resist the temptation to remove the cover so you don't lose your heat." He suggests presenting the fillet on a Hoyman-Browe platter. Hoyman-Browe is our local Mendocino County potter noted for their elegant, handcrafted earthenware pottery.

Parsley Mayonnaise

Yields: 1½ cups

- ⅓ **cup minced fresh Italian parsley**
- ⅓ **cup minced fresh cilantro**
- ¼ **cup minced green onions**
- 2 **tablespoons red wine vinegar**
- 1 **garlic clove, minced**
- ¼ **teaspoon dried oregano**
- ¼ **teaspoon freshly ground black pepper**
- ⅛ **teaspoon hot pepper sauce**
- 1 **cup mayonnaise**

Blend parsley, cilantro, green onions, vinegar, garlic, oregano, pepper, hot pepper sauce, and mayonnaise. Serve at room temperature right away or refrigerate overnight. Let stand at least 30 minutes to reach room temperature.

Although Mom developed this elegant topping to accompany the Baked Salmon with Herbed Crumb Topping, it would also be excellent with the John Moon and Jeanette's Cedar Plank Salmon recipe on page 128 or any baked or fried fish.

130

Open Face Shrimp Sandwich with Stroh Ranch Smoky Jalapeño Honey Sauce

Serves: 4

8   slices wheat bread
Mayonnaise
Spinach leaves
12   slices Cheddar cheese
3   tomatoes, sliced
2   packages (4 ounces each) alfalfa sprouts
3   avocados, sliced
1   pound cooked shrimp or crab
1   cup buttermilk ranch dressing
½   cup Mild Stroh Ranch Smoky Jalapeño Honey Sauce

This is a multi-layered sandwich. Cut 4 slices of bread into two triangles to be used for the 4 sandwiches. For the first sandwich, place a whole piece of bread on a large plate and place a triangle on the left side of this bread and place another triangle on the right side of the bread so the points are facing outward. Spread mayonnaise on all bread. Layer spinach leaves over mayonnaise. Place 3 slices of cheese over spinach. Top with tomato slices, a handful of sprouts, and avocado slices. Spread shrimp or crab on top. Blend dressing with jalapeño sauce. Drizzle sauce over sandwich. Make the other 3 sandwiches. Refrigerate until ready to serve. The leftover sauce is great on a taco salad, dinner salad, chef salad, or as a dip for artichokes and asparagus.

Our customers loved this lunch! It looks beautiful on a plate and tastes wonderful. For a little spicier flavor, you can use the Hot Stroh Ranch Smoky Jalapeño Honey Sauce (see www.pjsgourmet.com).

131

Scallop Cakes with Cilantro-Lime Mayonnaise   Serves: 4

Cilantro-Lime Mayonnaise

1   cup packed fresh cilantro leaves
3   tablespoons fresh lime juice
1   garlic clove, peeled
1   teaspoon Dijon mustard
1/4   teaspoon hot pepper sauce
3/4   cup mayonnaise
Salt and pepper to taste

Scallops

1   tablespoon olive oil
1   cup finely chopped onions
2   pounds sea scallops
1/2   cup chopped fresh chives
2   tablespoons chopped fresh parsley
2   tablespoons all-purpose flour
1   tablespoon minced fresh ginger
1   tablespoon fresh lime juice
1   large egg, beaten
2   teaspoons salt
1   teaspoon grated lime peel
3/4   teaspoon ground black pepper
2   tablespoons peanut oil
Whole chives and cilantro sprigs for garnish

To make the Cilantro-Lime Mayonnaise, blend cilantro, lime juice, garlic, mustard, and hot pepper sauce in a food processor until cilantro is finely chopped. Add mayonnaise and process just to blend. Transfer to a small bowl and add salt and pepper. Cover and refrigerate until ready to serve. Heat olive oil in medium nonstick skillet over medium heat. Add onions and sauté about 6 minutes until tender. Let cool. Place scallops in a food processor. Coarsely chop and transfer to a large bowl. Stir in onions, chives, parsley, flour, ginger, lime juice, egg, salt, lime peel, and pepper. Shape scallop mixture into eight 1/2-inch thick patties, each about 3 to 3 1/2-inches in diameter. Place scallop cakes on a baking sheet. Cover and refrigerate for 1 hour. Preheat oven to 450 degrees. Heat peanut oil in a large nonstick skillet over medium-high heat. Working in batches, brown scallop cakes about 2 minutes per side until browned. Transfer cakes to baking sheet. Bake about 7 minutes. Place 2 scallop cakes on each of four individual plates. Top with Cilantro-Lime Mayonnaise and garnish with whole chives and cilantro sprigs.

ENTRÉES

Our close friends, Conrad and Joezelle Cox of the Supper Club, shared this delicious recipe in honor of Mom. My husband, John, and I really enjoyed testing this recipe. I know Mom would have loved it! They suggest serving them with buttered new potatoes. The raw scallop cakes can be prepared 6 hours ahead.

"I've eaten Jeanette's Country Cooking appetizers for many years. She never ceases to amaze me with the way she can create fantastic dishes to feed hordes of people. Always tasty, easy to eat while walking around with a paper plate, always different for each occasion, always skillfully prepared and served. She's one of our area's greatest gems!"

Jeri Thurkow, *Main Street News*
May 1996

133

Gnocchi

Yields: 25 dozen

8   large baking potatoes
2   eggs, slightly beaten
1½ teaspoons salt
2½ cups all-purpose flour
Butter and Parmigiano cheese
**   for garnish**

Cook potatoes in salted boiling water about 40 minutes. Drain and peel potatoes. Place potatoes in a large bowl. Mash potatoes to an even, smooth consistency. When potatoes are tepid, beat in eggs and salt using a hand mixer. Slowly sift and stir in flour a little at a time with a spoon. Turn out dough onto a floured surface. Knead with extra flour until dough is elastic and smooth. Cut dough into 36 egg-sized pieces. Roll each dough piece on floured board or with palm of your hand until dough is finger-size rolls. Cut rolls into 1-inch or 1½-inch lengths. Bring 6 quarts of salted water to a boil. Add a few gnocchi at a time and cook 1 minute or until gnocchi float. Do not crowd gnocchi. Scoop out with a slotted spoon. Serve hot with butter and Parmigiano cheese or with your favorite spaghetti sauce or creamy Parmesan sauce.

This recipe came from our close friend, Arlene Colombini, who worked for Mom for many years. She was the lead on the jobs Mom did not attend. Mom would call her the morning after every job to see how everything went. I have always loved gnocchi and am thankful to have this delicious recipe. Arlene told me it came from a collection of Italian recipes from Yolanda Colombini.

134

Chile Rellenos with Sauce

Serves: 6

Sauce

¹/₂	cup chopped yellow onion
1	garlic clove, minced
1	tablespoon vegetable oil
2	tablespoons tomato paste
1	cup chopped tomatoes
1	can (14¹/₂ ounces) beef broth
1	teaspoon sugar
¹/₂	teaspoon salt
1	teaspoon vinegar
1	tablespoon all-purpose flour
2	tablespoons water

Chile Rellenos

12	Anaheim peppers
12	pieces Monterey Jack cheese
12	pieces Cheddar cheese
	All-purpose flour
1	cup egg whites, about 6 eggs
¹/₂	cup egg yolks, about 6 eggs
4	tablespoons butter, melted

For the sauce, sauté onions and garlic in oil. Add tomato paste and tomatoes. Simmer for 10 minutes. Add broth, sugar, salt, and vinegar. Simmer until tomatoes have cooked away. Purée mixture in a blender and return to a saucepan. In a small bowl, whisk flour with water. Whisk mixture into saucepan. Cook sauce until slightly thickened. Preheat oven to 350 degrees. Cut off tops of peppers and remove seeds by slicing down one side. Cook chilies in salted boiling water for 10 minutes. Drain. Place a piece of each cheese inside each pepper. Dust each chile with flour. Set aside. In a small bowl, beat egg whites until stiff peaks form. In another bowl, beat egg yolks. Stir into egg whites. Add cooled butter and mix well. Pour half of batter evenly on the bottom of an oiled 10x8x2-inch baking dish. Arrange stuffed chilies on top. Spoon remaining batter over chilies. Bake 15-20 minutes or until golden browned and thoroughly heated. Serve immediately with the sauce.

135

Leg of Lamb with Onion Gravy

Serves: 6

4	**pound boneless leg of lamb**
2	**yellow onions, peeled and sliced**
½	**cup water**
6	**baking potatoes, peeled and quartered**
2	**tablespoons cornstarch**
¼	**cup water**

Salt and pepper to taste

Preheat oven to 350 degrees. Place lamb in a deep roasting pan and bake for 30 minutes. Add onions and water. Bake an additional 30 minutes. Add potatoes and bake another hour or until potatoes are done. Remove lamb and potatoes and keep warm. To make gravy, pour pan drippings and onions into a saucepan. Be sure to get all the drippings by pouring a little water in the baking pan and scraping the bottom and sides. Pour this into the saucepan. Whisk together cornstarch and water. Whisk in cornstarch mixture. Bring to boil. Continue to add cornstarch until gravy thickens. The amount of cornstarch depends on amount of drippings. Add salt and pepper. Serve potatoes in a dish. Slice the lamb and serve with hot onion gravy.

This is my dad's absolutely favorite recipe. He loves the onions in the gravy served over the lamb and potatoes. If you like the leg of lamb with the bone in, I suggest using a 6-pound roast. Very rarely was there much left over from this meal!

136

ENTRÉES

Butter Topping for Steaks

Serves: 8

1   **tablespoon butter**

¼   **cup chopped shallots**

2   **teaspoons minced garlic**

7   **tablespoons butter, softened**

1   **tablespoon Worcestershire sauce**

2   **tablespoons dry mustard**

2   **tablespoons chopped fresh chives**

¼   **teaspoon salt**

¼   **teaspoon pepper**

Melt 1 tablespoon butter in heavy skillet. Sauté shallots and garlic for 1 minute on medium heat. Transfer to a small bowl. Add remaining 7 tablespoons butter, Worcestershire sauce, mustard, chives, salt, and pepper. Blend with fork. Using your hands, roll mixture into a log about 5-6 inches long. Roll the log in plastic wrap and refrigerate until firm. When ready to use, let stand at room temperature to let soften slightly. Cut butter roll into slices and place on top of warm steaks just before serving.

This is one of four delicious recipes that came from Mom's good friend and cook, Gary Venturi. Gary told me this recipe can be made ahead and kept in the freezer until needed. I tested it on barbecued rib-eye steaks and loved it. It is very rich and a little spicy — both qualities I love in a sauce!

137

Tartar Sauce

Serves: 6

1 cup mayonnaise
1½ teaspoons dried dill
2 tablespoons minced chives
½ teaspoon celery seed
1 teaspoon Worcestershire sauce
1 teaspoon dried parsley
2 tablespoons minced dill pickles
Dash of hot pepper sauce
2 garlic cloves, minced
4 teaspoons capers, minced

Combine mayonnaise, dill, chives, celery seed, Worcestershire sauce, parsley, pickles, hot pepper sauce, garlic, and capers in a small bowl. Refrigerate. Serve chilled with your favorite fish.

This tartar sauce beats all basic ones I have made. It has so many ingredients that blend well together. I love the capers!

ENTRÉES

Mustard-Caper Sauce

Yields: 1½ cups

3   tablespoons coarsely ground mustard

2   egg yolks, room temperature

1   small green onion, chopped

¼   teaspoon ground marjoram

2   tablespoons lemon juice

1   cup olive oil

½   cup whipping cream

1½ tablespoons capers, drained

Blend mustard, egg yolks, green onions, marjoram and lemon juice in a food processor. Slowly blend in oil. Add cream and capers. Serve over chicken and vegetables.

WOW! What an amazing sauce. Try it over chicken, broccoli, green beans, potatoes, and cauliflower or use as a dipping sauce for meat. I know you will love this sauce!

139

COUNTRY COOKING

Notes:

Vegetables

CONTENTS

Parmesan Vegetable Sauce

Serves: 6

1 package (8 ounces) cream cheese, softened
³/₄ cup evaporated milk
¹/₂ teaspoon salt
¹/₂ teaspoon garlic salt
¹/₄ cup Parmesan cheese

In a small, deep bowl, beat together cream cheese and milk with a hand mixer until smooth. Pour into a saucepan. Heat until hot. Add salt, garlic salt, and Parmesan cheese. Cook and stir until cheese melts and has a smooth consistency. Serve hot over baked potatoes or your favorite steamed vegetables.

This is another one of Pat Denny's amazing recipes. It is a rich sauce that tastes great on potatoes. My husband, John, and I think it would also be great over pasta and even as a fondue served with chunks of fresh sourdough bread.

143

Baked Asparagus with Parmesan and Almonds Serves: 8

½ **cup whole almonds**

½ **cup grated Parmesan cheese**

½ **teaspoon salt**

1½ **pounds asparagus, trimmed**

½ **cup butter**

Spread almonds on a baking sheet and bake at 350 degrees until lightly toasted. Coarsely chop almonds. Combine almonds, Parmesan cheese, and salt. Mix well. Plunge asparagus into salted boiling water. Cook until crisp-tender and bright green. Drain and immerse in cold water. Butter a shallow baking dish with 1 tablespoon of butter. Arrange asparagus in dish. Top with almond mixture. Dot with remaining butter. Bake at 450 degrees for 20 minutes.

Supper Club members Monte and Kay Hill shared this recipe in honor of Mom. It is delicious and easy to prepare. Kay told me it is well received by the Supper Club and other guests!

Sweet and Sour Baked Beans

Serves: 8

6 slices bacon, diced

½ yellow onion, sliced

3 tablespoons wine vinegar

¼ cup packed brown sugar

½ teaspoon garlic salt

1 tablespoon dry mustard

1 can (15.25 ounces) kidney beans, drained

1 can (16 ounces) baked beans

1 can (15 ounces) butter beans, drained

1 can (15.50 ounces) garbanzos, drained

Cook bacon until crispy. Remove bacon and set aside. Simmer onions, vinegar, brown sugar, garlic salt, and mustard in drippings for 20 minutes. Combine kidney beans, baked beans, butter beans, and garbanzos in a stockpot and slowly heat. Add onion mixture and reserved bacon. Cover and simmer for 30 minutes.

My mom made large amounts of this recipe for her customers all summer long. Everyone loved it when we served it with our barbecued tri-tip. It is a unique recipe because of the variety of beans in it. The mix of beans is perfect with a wonderful sweet flavor.

Dr. C's Picnic Beans

Serves: 10

8-10 slices bacon, diced
1 medium onion, chopped
1 pound ground beef
⅓ cup ketchup
⅓ cup mild barbecue sauce
2½ tablespoons prepared yellow mustard
2½ tablespoons dark molasses
2 tablespoons chili powder
¼ teaspoon pepper
¼ teaspoon garlic salt
½ teaspoon minced garlic
1 can (16 ounces) dark red kidney beans, drained
1 can (16 ounces) pork and beans
1 can (16 ounces) butter beans

Fry bacon until crisp in a large frying pan. Reserve 2 tablespoons of drippings in the pan. Drain bacon on paper towels. Set aside. Brown onions in drippings until tender. Add ground beef and cook thoroughly. Add ketchup, barbecue sauce, mustard, molasses, chili powder, pepper, garlic salt, and garlic. Mix well. Add kidney beans, pork and beans, and butter beans and mix well. Stir in bacon and cook until boiling. Serve hot.

What a great recipe to test in the spring! We enjoyed it with barbecued hamburgers and hot dogs on a warm, sunny day. I tested it with our Mild Stroh Ranch Smoky Jalapeño Honey Sauce, but any barbecue sauce would taste fine. This chili is thick and slightly spicy from the chili powder. The recipe came from my sister's very special friend, Dr. Christison, who enjoyed cooking as much as Mom. My Mom loved this recipe and made it for family and friends.

146

Oriental Green Beans

Serves: 4

1 pound green beans, trimmed

4 teaspoons soy sauce

2½ tablespoons rice vinegar

1 tablespoon vegetable oil

1 large garlic clove, pressed

1 teaspoon fresh minced ginger

2 tablespoons chopped green onions

⅓ cup fresh cilantro leaves, chopped

¼ cup whole roasted and salted almonds

Cook green beans in boiling water for 10 minutes or until done. Immerse beans in cold water, drain and set aside. In a small bowl, combine soy sauce, rice vinegar, oil, garlic, ginger, green onions, and cilantro. In a large bowl, toss dressing with beans. Sprinkle with almonds. Marinate for 3 hours before serving. Serve at room temperature.

We are so thankful to our family friend, Karen Moon, for sharing this recipe with Mom many years ago. This is a great summer recipe when green beans are at their best. The flavors are intense and make you want to come back for more. The beans are tasty the next day too so you may want to make a larger amount for leftovers.

Corn Soufflé

Serves: 8

½ cup butter, melted

2 eggs, beaten

1 can (14¾ ounces) cream-style corn

4 ears corn, kernels cut off

1 container (8 ounces) sour cream

1 box (8.5 ounces) cornbread mix

Preheat oven to 325 degrees. Combine butter, eggs, cream-style corn, whole corn, sour cream, and cornbread mix. Pour mixture into a 13x9x2-inch baking dish. Bake for 45 minutes.

This recipe was printed in our local paper, the Ukiah Daily Journal, in 1984. A writer did a story about Mom on ranching and cooking, and Mom decided to give the paper some of her favorite corn recipes to print.

Fresh Corn and Zucchini

Serves: 8

4	**tablespoons butter**
½	**cup thinly sliced yellow onions**
4	**ears corn, kernels cut off**
3	**cups diced Roma tomatoes**
1	**pound zucchini, sliced**
1	**teaspoon salt**
Pepper to taste	
¼	**cup chopped parsley**

Melt butter in a sauté pan and add the onion. Cook onions until tender but not browned. Add whole corn, tomatoes, zucchini, salt, and pepper. Cover and cook 10 minutes. Sprinkle with parsley and serve hot as a side dish.

We enjoyed eating our fresh sweet corn and vegetables from our 1-acre garden on the ranch. Tomatoes, corn and zucchini grew beautifully in our soil. This recipe was printed in the Ukiah Daily Journal on October 23, 1984 for a cover story on the ranch and Mom's cooking. It is a colorful side dish that all of our tasters enjoyed with a prime rib dinner.

Fresh Corn Cakes
Serves: 8

2 cups all-purpose flour
2½ tablespoons sugar
2 teaspoons baking powder
1½ teaspoons salt
¼ teaspoon pepper
3 eggs
¾ cup milk
2 tablespoons butter, melted
4 ears fresh sweet corn, kernels cut off
Canola oil

In a large bowl, combine flour, sugar, baking powder, salt, and pepper. In a separate bowl, beat eggs until thick. Blend in milk and butter until well mixed. Whisk into flour mixture. Stir in corn. Add more milk if batter is too thick. Generously oil a frying pan or griddle. Heat the pan. Drop batter by tablespoon onto pan. Cook cakes about 3 minutes until bubbly and browned around the edges. Flip and cook until browned. May need more oil after cooking each batch. Serve warm with butter.

These make a wonderful side dish with a roast. This recipe was printed in the Ukiah Daily Journal on October 23, 1984. They did a cover story on Mom because of the wonderful sweet corn we grew for our produce stand and local markets. Mom was always trying to find ways to cook the sweet corn, and I think this recipe was a great idea.

150

Zucchini Pancakes   Serves: 6

2   medium zucchini, grated
1   package (8 ounces)
**   shredded sharp Cheddar**
**   cheese**
½   teaspoon salt
½   teaspoon pepper
1   small onion, finely chopped
1   garlic clove, chopped
2   eggs
½   cup biscuit baking mix
2   tablespoons butter

Combine zucchini, Cheddar cheese, salt, pepper, onions, garlic, eggs, and biscuit mix in a medium bowl. Melt butter in a large hot frying pan. Drop batter by heaping tablespoons into hot frying pan. Cook until golden browned on both sides. Serve warm.

Mom loved this recipe. We tried it at a dinner party at Mom and Dad's house several years ago, and they were a hit with our family. My husband, John, who does not like zucchini, let us know he will only eat zucchini in these pancakes! They look beautiful on a dinner plate.

151

Chile Relleno Casserole   Serves: 6

2 cans (4 ounces each) whole green chilies

2 eggs

1 cup milk

½ cup all-purpose flour

½ teaspoon salt

1 package (8 ounces) shredded Monterey Jack cheese

Preheat oven to 350 degrees. Cut chilies to open flat. Scrape out seeds. Place chilies on the bottom of an 8x8x2-inch buttered baking dish. In a bowl, beat eggs. Stir in milk, flour, and salt. Add three-fourths cheese. Pour milk mixture over chilies. Sprinkle remaining cheese on top. Bake for 45 minutes.

The whole chilies taste wonderful. This is a quick recipe to put together compared to the Chile Rellenos with Sauce. I would use this more as a side dish than an entrée.

152

Vegetable Soufflé

Serves: 8

3 cups chopped spinach or
2 cups chopped zucchini
or broccoli

1 can (10¾ ounces) cream of
mushroom soup

1 cup mayonnaise

1 cup shredded Monterey
Jack cheese

1 cup shredded Cheddar
cheese

¼ cup chopped white onion
or shallot

3 eggs, beaten

Preheat oven to 350 degrees. Cook desired vegetable in a small amount of boiling water about 2-4 minutes until just tender. Drain. In a large bowl, combine soup, mayonnaise, Jack cheese, Cheddar cheese, onions, and eggs. Stir in cooked vegetables. Pour mixture into a lightly greased 13x9x2-inch baking dish. Bake for 40 minutes or until set and a knife inserted in the center comes out clean. Let stand for 5 minutes before serving.

This was one of Mom's most popular vegetable dishes. It paired so well with everything, from barbecued tri-tip and chicken to baked pork loins. My favorite way to serve it is with the chopped zucchini.

153

Roasted Autumn Vegetables

Serves: 6

1   medium acorn squash, peeled, seeded and cubed

2   large yams, peeled and cubed

4   large red potatoes, cubed

¼   cup butter or margarine, melted

Garlic salt, salt, and pepper to taste

2   teaspoons dried parsley

Preheat oven to 350 degrees. Arrange squash, yams, and potatoes on a large baking sheet. Toss with butter. Sprinkle with garlic salt, salt, and pepper. Sprinkle with parsley. Bake about 40 minutes, turning vegetables occasionally, until evenly golden crispy browned.

I love the variety of roasted vegetables in this recipe. It's so easy to just use potatoes, but adding the yams and acorn squash gives color, interesting texture, and flavor. I have even added turnips and rutabagas for more variety.

154

Red Potatoes with Bacon and Buttermilk Dressing

Serves: 6

2½	**pounds red potatoes**
1	**package (0.4 ounces) dry buttermilk dressing mix**
1	**cup buttermilk**
1	**cup mayonnaise**
8-10	**slices bacon, diced and cooked crisp**
1	**bunch green onions, chopped**

Cook potatoes in boiling water about 45-50 minutes or until tender. Drain. Cool potatoes completely. Slice into ¼-inch thick rounds and set aside. In a small bowl, blend dressing mix, buttermilk, and mayonnaise. Spread one-fourth dressing mixture evenly on the bottom of an 8x8x2-baking dish. Arrange one-third potato rounds evenly over dressing. Sprinkle one-third bacon and green onions evenly over potatoes. Repeat layering of all ingredients in same order. Remaining dressing will be last layer on top. Bake at 350 degrees about 30 minutes until hot.

This is my favorite scalloped potato recipe! Our catering customers loved it too and always asked for it to pair with our barbecued tri-tips. It is a very easy recipe to make and looks pretty on a plate full of Mom's food.

155

Mary Louise's Shredded Potatoes

Serves: 8

8 **baking potatoes, cooked and cooled**

½ **cup butter**

1 **package (8 ounces) shredded sharp Cheddar cheese**

⅓ **cup sliced green onions**

1 **pint sour cream**

½ **teaspoon salt**

½ **teaspoon pepper**

Preheat oven to 350 degrees. Peel cooled potatoes. Grate into a large bowl. Stir in butter, Cheddar cheese, green onions, sour cream, salt, and pepper. Pour mixture into a 13x9x2-inch baking dish. Bake for 30 minutes. Serve as a side dish for dinner.

Our close family friend, Mary Louise Chase, served this to Mom at one of her fun dinner parties and it became a big hit with our family. Mary Louise always cools the cooked potatoes before grating them. It is much easier that way.

156

Creamy Stuffed Potatoes   Serves: 4

4 baking potatoes
Canola oil
¹/₂ cup sour cream
¹/₄ cup milk
1 teaspoon salt
1 tablespoon chopped parsley
1 tablespoon chopped green onion
Pepper to taste
¹/₄ cup plus 4 tablespoons grated Cheddar cheese

Preheat oven to 400 degrees. Wash and scrub even-sized baking potatoes. Dry potatoes and brush each entirely with oil. Bake 50 minutes-1 hour until tender. Cut potatoes lengthwise and scoop out pulp. Set shells aside. Mash potato pulp in a bowl. Stir in sour cream, milk, salt, parsley, green onions, pepper, and ¹/₄ cup Cheddar cheese. Mix well. Divide mixture evenly into 4 shells. Top each with 1 tablespoon Cheddar cheese. Bake at 350 degrees 15 minutes or until potatoes are very hot and cheese melts.

Mom enjoyed serving these as a change from the huge amount of potato salad she made. She usually served these with barbecued tri-tip or prime rib.

157

Spanakopita

Serves: 10

½ **small onion, chopped**
1 **garlic clove, chopped**
1 **tablespoon olive oil**
1 **package (10 ounces) frozen spinach, thawed and squeezed dry**
¼ **cup grated Parmesan cheese**
2 **packages (8 ounces each) cream cheese, softened**
1 **egg**
1 **tablespoon milk**
¼ **teaspoon salt**
¼ **teaspoon pepper**
1 **package (16 ounces) frozen phyllo dough, thawed in refrigerator**
½ **cup butter, melted**
1 **cup unseasoned bread crumbs**

Preheat oven to 325 degrees. Sauté onions and garlic in oil and set aside. Combine spinach and Parmesan cheese. In a food processor, blend cream cheese, egg, and milk until creamy. Add to spinach mixture. Stir in onions, garlic, salt, and pepper. Mix thoroughly and set aside. Place two phyllo sheets on the bottom of a 13x9x2-inch baking dish. Brush with butter. Sprinkle with some bread crumbs. Layer two more phyllo sheets on top. Brush with butter. Sprinkle with some bread crumbs. Place two more phyllo sheets on top. Brush with butter. Sprinkle with bread crumbs. Spread some spinach mixture evenly on top. Place two phyllo sheets over spinach. Brush with butter and sprinkle with breadcrumbs. Repeat spinach mixture, phyllo sheets, butter, and bread crumbs layers two more times. Bake until lightly browned. Cut into squares and serve warm.

I love the flaky texture of this Greek side dish. I learned to work quickly with the phyllo dough. The trick is to make sure it does not dry out too much as you are making this dish. Take two sheets out and cover the remaining phyllo dough with plastic wrap until you are ready for the next two sheets.

Zucchini Frittata

Serves: 8

3 cups sliced zucchini

½ onion

1 tablespoon chopped fresh parsley

1 garlic clove

1 cup biscuit baking mix

½ cup vegetable oil

½ teaspoon seasoned salt

½ cup grated Parmesan cheese

4 eggs

Pepper to taste

Preheat oven to 350 degrees. Blend zucchini, onions, parsley, and garlic in a food processor. Add baking mix, oil, seasoned salt, Parmesan cheese, eggs, and pepper. Blend to a smooth consistency. Pour mixture into a 13x9x2-inch baking dish. Bake 40 minutes. Serve hot.

Mom loved finding recipes that used zucchini. This one is easy to make with everything blended in the food processor.

COUNTRY COOKING

Notes:

Pasta
&
Rice

CONTENTS

John's Spaghetti Sauce

Serves: 8

4	tablespoons olive oil
2	medium yellow onions, chopped
2	pounds cooked Polish or smoked sausages, sliced into 1/2-inch rounds
1	medium sweet red pepper, chopped
3	large stalks celery, diced
2	medium carrots, grated
3	medium ripe red tomatoes, cubed
1	can (15 ounces) tomato sauce
1	can (6 ounces) tomato paste
1	can (14.5 ounces) Italian style stewed tomatoes with juice
2	cans (2.25 ounces each) sliced black olives, drained
3/4	cup red wine
1/2	teaspoon salt
1/4	teaspoon freshly ground pepper

Parmesan cheese for garnish

This recipe is best if made the night or morning before serving. Heat oil in a large stockpot. Sauté onions over medium high heat until golden browned. Add sausage and sauté until browned. Reduce heat. Stir in peppers, celery, and carrots. Cook for 2 minutes. Add tomatoes, tomato sauce, tomato paste, stewed tomatoes, olives, wine, salt, and pepper. Cover and bring to a slow boil, stirring occasionally. Remove from heat and let cool. Reheat slowly and simmer for 1 hour before serving. Serve over cooked, thin spaghetti with Parmesan cheese sprinkled on top.

This is my husband's signature dish. It is unique with the carrots hidden inside. He loves eating it with garlic bread, green salad, Zinfandel wine, and my apple pie. He suggests using stronger red wine for the sauce such as a Cabernet Sauvignon or Zinfandel.

163

Basil Spaghetti

Serves: 8

1 garlic bulb, pulled apart, peeled and minced

½ cup chopped fresh basil leaves

½ cup chopped fresh parsley

½ cup butter

1 package (16 ounces) thin spaghetti noodles

Salt to taste

½ cup Parmesan cheese

Sauté garlic, basil, and parsley in butter. Do not boil. Cook spaghetti according to package directions. Drain pasta and pour into a large pasta bowl. Add salt, garlic sauce and toss with Parmesan cheese. Serve warm.

If you like garlic, you will love this recipe. We would always laugh that it's not a clove of garlic but one whole bulb in this recipe! Sometimes Mom would use green spaghetti noodles to show off the garlic.

164

Father Gary Noodles

Serves: 8

2	**bunches basil leaves, roughly chopped**
4	**cups diced tomatoes**
10	**garlic cloves, chopped**
½	**cup olive oil**
1½	**teaspoons salt**
Pepper to taste	
1	**package (16 ounces) fusilli pasta**

Simmer basil, tomatoes, garlic, oil, salt, and pepper in a covered stockpot for 1 hour. Cook pasta according to package directions. Drain. Pour sauce over cooked pasta and serve hot.

This was a favorite of our catering customers. Father Gary, from our local Catholic Church, shared this recipe with Mom. He loved Mom's cooking! The recipe can be made ahead and easily reheated for leftovers.

165

Vegetarian Lasagna

Serves: 8

½ package (16 ounces) lasagna, 9 noodles

1 package (10 ounces) frozen chopped spinach, thawed and squeezed dry

1 jar (25 ounces) marinara sauce

¼ cup red wine

1 teaspoon garlic salt

½ teaspoon salt

3 cups shredded Monterey Jack cheese

3 cups shredded Cheddar cheese

1 teaspoon dried parsley

Parmesan cheese for garnish

Cook lasagna noodles according to package directions. Cool and set aside. Place spinach in a large bowl. Add marinara sauce, red wine, garlic salt, and salt. Mix well. In a medium bowl, combine two cheeses and set aside. You will make 3 layers of lasagna. Spread one-fourth sauce evenly on the bottom of a 13x9x2-inch baking dish. Top evenly with 3 noodles. Spread sauce over noodles. Sprinkle 1 ½ cups cheese mixture evenly over sauce. Cover with 3 noodles. Spread sauce over noodles. Sprinkle 1 ½ cups cheese mixture over sauce. Top with remaining 3 noodles. Spoon remaining sauce over noodles. Sprinkle with remaining cheese mixture. Top with parsley. Bake at 350 degrees 40 minutes or until heated through and golden browned. Serve hot with Parmesan cheese.

This is a very simple recipe and very tasty. Mom didn't enjoy the fancy lasagnas. She liked the ingredients to be basic and easy to put together. This was a very popular dish to serve for people at catering events who did not eat meat.

166

Meat Lasagna   Serves: 8

½ **package (16 ounces) lasagna, 9 noodles**
1   **pound ground beef**
1   **jar (25 ounces) marinara sauce**
¼ **cup red wine**
1   **teaspoon garlic salt**
½ **teaspoon salt**
3   **cups shredded Monterey Jack cheese**
3   **cups shredded Cheddar cheese**
1   **teaspoon dried parsley**
Parmesan cheese for garnish

Cook lasagna according to package directions. Cool and set aside. Brown meat until crumbly. Drain drippings. Place meat in a large bowl. Add marinara sauce, red wine, garlic salt, and salt. Mix well. In a medium bowl, combine two cheeses. Set aside. You will make 3 layers of lasagna. Spread one-fourth of meat sauce evenly on the bottom of a 13x9x2-inch baking dish. Top with 3 noodles. Spread sauce over noodles. Sprinkle 1 ½ cups cheese mixture evenly over sauce. Cover with 3 noodles. Spread sauce over noodles. Sprinkle 1 ½ cups cheese mixture over sauce. Top with remaining 3 noodles. Spread remaining sauce over noodles. Sprinkle with remaining cheese mixture. Top with parsley. Bake at 350 degrees 40 minutes or until heated through and golden browned. Serve hot with Parmesan cheese.

Both of her lasagna recipes are similar. This recipe only changed by replacing the spinach with ground beef. Throughout the year she would serve this to her catering customers and also made this recipe into mini lasagnas and sold them "to go" to our local pizzeria, Pizza Etc.

167

COUNTRY COOKING

Pasta Salad Supreme
Serves: 10

1 **pound vermicelli, broken in half**

1 **package (0.7 ounces) dry Italian salad dressing mix**

4½ **tablespoons salad supreme seasoning**

2 **green onions, minced**

3 **Roma tomatoes, diced**

1 **can (2.25 ounces) sliced olives**

¼ **cup olive oil**

Cook pasta according to package directions. Drain and cool. Pour pasta into a large bowl. Add dressing mix, seasoning, green onions, tomatoes, olives, and oil. Mix well until the seasonings are evenly distributed through the pasta. Refrigerate. Serve chilled as a side dish in a low pasta bowl.

Mom started making this pasta for our family in 1983. Sometimes we would add fresh vegetables from the garden including minced squash and chopped sweet red and bell peppers. It looks beautiful with a variety of vegetables and has a wonderful tangy flavor. Mom would sometimes serve it with about 4 tablespoons minced red onions in place of the green onions.

Macaroni Salad

Serves: 8

1 **package (16 ounces) macaroni pasta or small seashells**

3 **hard-cooked eggs, chopped**

1/2 **teaspoon garlic salt**

3/4 **teaspoon seasoned salt**

3/4 **teaspoon pepper**

3 **tablespoons chopped red onions**

4 **teaspoons dried parsley**

2 **cups real mayonnaise**

Cook macaroni according to package directions. Drain pasta and cool completely in a large bowl. Add eggs, garlic salt, seasoned salt, pepper, red onions, parsley, and mayonnaise. Mix well. Refrigerate until ready to serve.

This is the recipe Mom made for the local delis in Mendocino County. I love the basic ingredients with the sweet of the red onion.

169

Campanelle Pasta Salad

Serves: 12

Pasta

1 package (16 ounces) campanelle pasta
1 cup chopped green onions
1 can (5 ¾ ounces) whole, pitted black olives, drained
1 cup sliced green olives
2 cups cherry tomatoes
1 cup frozen artichoke hearts, thawed and chopped
2 cups frozen peas, thawed

Dressing

½ cup chopped yellow onion
4 garlic cloves
1 ½ teaspoons dry mustard
1 ½ teaspoons salt
3 tablespoons sugar
3 tablespoons water
¾ teaspoon pepper

1 cup olive oil
½ cup cider vinegar
1 teaspoon dried basil
1 teaspoon dried oregano
1 cup Parmesan cheese

Cook pasta according to package directions. Drain and let cool. In a large bowl, combine pasta, green onions, black olives, green olives, tomatoes, artichokes, and peas. Blend onions, garlic, mustard, salt, sugar, water, pepper, oil, vinegar, basil, and oregano in a food processor. Pour dressing over pasta and toss lightly. Refrigerate 2 hours. Before serving, toss with Parmesan cheese.

Our close friend, Mary Louise Chase, shared this recipe with Mom. The flavors of this recipe are incredible with a hint of sweet. We had many tasters try it and everyone loved it. Our friend, Norma Dunsing, likes to also add chopped fresh basil and a basil bouquet on the top of the salad to add to the presentation of this beautiful pasta dish.

Pasta and Vegetable Salad

Serves: 12

Salad

1/3 cup pine nuts
1 teaspoon butter, melted
1 package (8 ounces) fusilli pasta
8 ounces sliced mushrooms
2 cans (2.25 ounces each) sliced black olives, drained
1/4 cup sliced green olives with pimento
2 jars (6 ounces each) marinated artichoke hearts, drained and quartered
1 sweet red pepper, chopped
1 can (15 ounces) garbanzo beans, drained
1 package (10 ounces) frozen petite peas, thawed
2 medium zucchini, sliced
1 1/4 pounds chicken, cooked and diced

Dressing

1/2 cup olive oil
2 tablespoons red wine vinegar
2 teaspoons Dijon mustard
1/8 teaspoon curry powder
1/4 cup chopped fresh parsley
1/2 teaspoon salt
1/4 teaspoon pepper

Combine pine nuts and butter. Toast at 350 degrees until lightly toasted. Set aside. Cook pasta according to package directions. Drain pasta and set aside. In a large bowl, combine mushrooms, black olives, green olives, artichokes, peppers, beans, peas, zucchini, and chicken. Blend oil, vinegar, mustard, curry, parsley, salt, and pepper. Pour dressing over chicken mixture. Add pasta and pine nuts and toss lightly. Refrigerate overnight and serve at room temperature.

Our wonderful friends, Carol and Roy Stokes, shared this delicious recipe with Mom. It is a beautiful salad with a light dressing.

171

Raul's Jalapeño White Rice

Serves: 10

½ **cup butter**

4 **cups chicken broth**

3 **garlic cloves, halved**

1 **large jalapeño pepper, trimmed, seeded and halved**

¼ **yellow onion, thinly sliced**

2 **cups uncooked white rice**

Melt butter in broth in a saucepan. Add garlic, jalapeño, and onions. Bring to boil. Add rice. Cover and simmer over low heat 30 minutes or until rice is fluffy. Serve hot.

My nephew, Kenny Madigan, loves this rice. Every time he visited the ranch he would walk down to the kitchen and ask Raul if he could make this white rice, even early in the morning. When I tried it for the first time recently, I thought it was definitely good enough to have in the cookbook. The jalapeño is added just for flavor; you can take it out of the rice before serving. If you want a little more heat to it, just add more sliced jalapeño peppers.

PASTA & RICE

Raul's Red Rice

Serves: 15

1	can (8 ounces) tomato paste
3	Roma tomatoes
½	yellow onion, halved
3	garlic cloves, halved
3	cups long grain white rice, uncooked
½	cup olive oil
2	jalapeños peppers, halved, trimmed and seeded
6	cups chicken broth

Purée tomato paste, tomatoes, onions, and garlic in a food processor. Set aside. Cook rice in oil until lightly browned. Pour tomato mixture over rice and add jalapeños. Cook for 1 minute. Pour broth over rice and simmer about 30-40 minutes until liquid is absorbed. Serve hot with tacos or enchiladas.

Be sure to cover the pot while the rice is simmering. Enjoy!

This makes a huge amount of Raul's authentic red rice. I kept the recipe the same as he made it when he worked for Mom. He made this in large restaurant pans in the commercial kitchen. You may want to cut the recipe in half for smaller parties. The leftover rice is great over the next couple of days in tacos and with eggs.

173

Southwestern Wild Rice and Olive Salad   Serves: 6

Salad

2½ cups cooked wild rice

¾ cup drained black olives, sliced

½ cup canned corn

½ cup chopped sweet red pepper

½ cup chopped Roma tomatoes

¼ cup sliced green onions

2 tablespoons chopped cilantro

1 tablespoon chopped jalapeño pepper

Salt and pepper to taste

Dressing

⅓ cup sour cream

2 tablespoons olive oil

1 tablespoon lime juice

1 tablespoon ground cumin

Combine wild rice, olives, corn, peppers, tomatoes, green onions, cilantro, jalapeños, salt, and pepper in a bowl. Blend sour cream, oil, lime juice, and cumin. Pour dressing over rice. Mix well. Serve at room temperature.

What fun it was to test this one. It finishes so colorful and delicious. It had two thumbs up from both my dad and husband. For added flavor, my mom would cook the wild rice with two chicken bouillon cubes to make the 2½ cups cooked rice.

174

Barley Casserole with Pine Nuts and Oyster Mushrooms

Serves: 12

1   **cup pine nuts**
1   **pound oyster mushrooms, sliced**
Olive oil
2   **cups barley**
1   **large yellow onion, chopped**
¼   **cup butter**
½   **cup minced green onions**
1   **teaspoon garlic salt**
½   **teaspoon pepper**
7   **cups warm chicken broth**
½   **cup lightly chopped Italian parsley**

Preheat oven to 375 degrees. Toast pine nuts, until lightly browned. Set aside. Sauté mushrooms in oil until slightly limp and set aside. Rinse and drain barley. Sauté barley and onions in butter in a large pan until barley is slightly browned. Add green onions, garlic salt, pepper, broth, pine nuts, and mushrooms into the pan. Mix well. Pour mixture into a 13x9x2-inch baking dish. Bake for 1 hour. Garnish with parsley.

This is a hearty recipe that will fill you up quickly. Mom used this recipe often during the winter months for larger catering jobs. I saw a note where she multiplied this recipe by 10! The oyster mushrooms and green onions are a delicious addition.

175

COUNTRY COOKING

Notes:

Desserts

CONTENTS

178

Pear Dutch Baby

Serves: 6

Fruit Filling

4   **Bosc pears, cored and sliced**
½   **cup packed brown sugar**
½   **cup lemon juice**
Water
1   **tablespoon all-purpose flour**

Dutch Baby

3   **tablespoons butter**
1   **cup all-purpose flour**
3   **tablespoons sugar**
¼   **teaspoon salt**
3   **large eggs**
1   **cup milk**
Powdered sugar

Preheat oven to 425 degrees. Combine sliced pears, brown sugar, and lemon juice in a saucepan. Sauté 10 minutes. With a slotted spoon, remove pears from the juice and set aside, reserving juice in the pan. In a small bowl, mix a little water with flour until creamy but not thick. Heat juice in the pan. Slowly whisk flour mixture into the hot juice and cook until thickened. Return pears to juice and keep warm. To make the Dutch Baby, melt butter in a 10-inch oven proof skillet over medium heat. Blend flour, sugar, salt, eggs, and milk in a food processor. Pour batter into skillet. Cook 20 minutes or until puffy and browned. Place on a round platter. Spoon warm pear mixture into the center of the pancake. Sprinkle with powdered sugar. Cut into 6 wedges and serve immediately with a scoop of vanilla ice cream.

I enjoy the texture of this giant pancake mixed with the tart mixture of pear and lemon. I had never heard of a Dutch baby until I found Mom's recipe. The batter is fun to watch as it bakes. It goes up the sides of the pan, and you may get a bubble or two in the middle. It looks so beautiful when it is finished with the powdered sugar on top.

179

Bread Pudding

Serves: 8

Bread Pudding

7   slices raisin bread, cut into small cubes

3   slices sweet French bread, cut into small cubes

5   eggs

2   cups whipping cream

½   cup butter, melted

1   teaspoon vanilla

½   teaspoon cinnamon

Whiskey Sauce

1   cup sugar

½   cup water

3   tablespoons plus 1 teaspoon cornstarch

¼   cup butter

½   teaspoon cinnamon

3   tablespoons whiskey or brandy

Preheat oven to 325 degrees. Spread cubed bread evenly in the bottom of a 13x9x2-inch baking dish. Blend eggs, whipping cream, butter, vanilla, and cinnamon. Pour mixture over the bread and lightly toss until bread is moistened. Pour ½ inch warm water in a pan larger than the 13x9x2-inch baking dish. Place pudding dish inside larger pan to make a water bath. Cover pudding with foil. Bake for 40 minutes. Uncover and bake another 20 minutes until lightly browned. For the whiskey sauce, whisk sugar and water together in a saucepan over medium heat until the sugar dissolves. Whisk in cornstarch. Add butter and cinnamon. Cook and stir over medium heat until thickened. Stir in whiskey or brandy and cook another 5 minutes. Cut bread pudding into 8 servings. Place in a bowl or on small plates. Generously spoon the whiskey sauce over the bread pudding and serve warm.

Long ago, people made bread pudding as a common way to use up stale bread. Today we consider it a delicious treat. The whiskey sauce really adds to this recipe. You may even want to add a little more whiskey to taste. I was a little conservative.

DESSERTS

No Bake Pumpkin Cheesecake   Serves: 10

Crust

20 gingersnaps, crushed
½ cup pecans, chopped
⅓ cup butter, melted

Filling

1 envelope (¼ ounce)
unflavored gelatin
¼ cup boiling water
20 ounces cream cheese,
softened
½ cup sugar
¾ cup canned pumpkin
2¼ teaspoons pumpkin spice

Combine gingersnaps, pecans, and butter. Press mixture into a 9½-inch pie plate. Dissolve gelatin in water and set aside. Blend cream cheese, sugar, pumpkin, and pumpkin spice in a food processor. Stir in gelatin. Spoon filling into prepared crust. Refrigerate 2-3 hours. Serve chilled.

I loved the no bake cheesecake idea when I tested this recipe. Mom had made this before, but I had never tried it. It is very rich and thickens nicely with the gelatin. The pumpkin flavor is not overpowering and the gingersnap crust adds a fun twist to the traditional graham cracker crust.

181

Chocolate and Pistachio Paté with Cream   Serves: 16

Paté

1½   cups shelled, unsalted
      pistachios
18   ounces semi-sweet
      chocolate chips
2¼   cups unsalted butter,
      softened
3   cups unsweetened cocoa
      powder
1   cup sugar
½   cup water
6   egg yolks
3   eggs
¼   cup Grand Marnier or other
      orange liqueur
2   tablespoons vanilla

Pistachio Cream Sauce

1½   cups whipping cream
6   egg yolks
½   cup sugar
1   teaspoon vanilla
2   tablespoons finely chopped,
      shelled unsalted pistachios
Mint leaves and raspberries for
      garnish

Line a 9x5-inch glass loaf pan with parchment paper. Place pistachios on a baking sheet and bake at 350 degrees until lightly toasted. Set aside. Melt chocolate, butter, and cocoa in the top of a double boiler over gently simmering water. Stir until smooth. Transfer to a large bowl and cool slightly. Cook sugar and water in a heavy small saucepan over low heat, stirring constantly, until sugar dissolves. Increase heat and simmer syrup about 4 minutes. Whisk together egg yolks, eggs, liqueur, and vanilla in a medium bowl. Stir syrup into the chocolate mixture. Fold in nuts. Whisk egg mixture into chocolate mixture. Pour mixture into prepared mold. Cover with plastic wrap and refrigerate overnight. For the cream sauce, bring cream to boil in a heavy saucepan. Whisk together egg yolks, sugar, and vanilla in a large bowl. Gradually whisk hot cream into egg mixture. Return mixture to saucepan. Stir over medium-low heat about

DESSERTS

10 minutes until mixture thickens and leaves path on back of spoon when finger is drawn across. Be careful not to let it curdle with too much heat. Fill a large bowl with ice. Place a smaller bowl inside ice bowl. Using a strainer with very small holes, strain cream sauce into the small bowl. Cool completely over ice while stirring frequently. Add nuts. Cover and refrigerate. Cut paté into thin slices. Spoon the pistachio cream sauce onto dessert plates. Arrange paté slices over sauce. Place a mint leaf on the side and top with raspberries.

This recipe came from Chef Ken Dunn at the American Restaurant in Kansas City, Missouri. This recipe had special ties to Mom because that is the town where she was born. Her clients loved this decadent and rich dessert.

Chocolate Delight

Serves: 12

½ cup butter, melted
1 cup all-purpose flour
½ cup finely chopped nuts
4 packages (3 ounces each) cream cheese, softened
½ cup powdered sugar
½ teaspoon vanilla
2 packages (3 ounces each) instant chocolate pudding mix
3½ cups milk
1 container (8 ounces) frozen whipped topping, thawed

Preheat oven to 350 degrees. This makes a four-layer dessert. Combine butter, flour, and nuts in a bowl. Press mixture evenly onto the bottom of a 13x9x2-inch baking dish. Bake about 15 minutes or until lightly browned. Let cool. Blend cream cheese, powdered sugar, and vanilla in a bowl. Spread mixture evenly over cooled bottom. Add a little milk to reach spreading consistency. Whisk together pudding mix and milk. Pour over cream cheese layer. Refrigerate until set. Top with whipped topping. Refrigerate. Serve chilled.

Variations:

Lemon Delight:
For the third layer, replace chocolate pudding with 2 small packages instant lemon pudding mix. Blend with milk and pour over the second layer. Top with whipped topping.

Banana Cream Delight:
For the third layer, replace chocolate pudding with 2 small packages instant banana pudding mix. Blend with milk and pour over the second layer. Top with whipped topping. You may want to add some banana slices to pudding.

Pumpkin Delight:
For the third layer, replace chocolate pudding with 2 small packages instant vanilla pudding mix and add 1 small can pumpkin, 1 teaspoon cinnamon, ½ teaspoon ground ginger, and ½ teaspoon ground cloves. Use 2 cups milk instead of 3. Blend with milk and pour over the second layer. Top with whipped topping.

Cheesecake

Serves: 10

Crust

16 graham crackers, crushed
½ cup sugar
⅓ cup butter, melted

Filling

2 packages (8 ounces each) cream cheese, softened
2 eggs
½ cup sugar
1 teaspoon vanilla

Topping

1 cup sour cream
3 tablespoons sugar

Preheat oven to 350 degrees. Combine cracker crumbs, sugar, and butter. Press mixture into the bottom and up sides of a 9-inch pie plate. Bake for 10 minutes. Decrease oven to 325 degrees. Blend cream cheese, eggs, sugar, and vanilla in a food processor. Pour filling into crust. Bake 20 minutes or until set. Whisk together sour cream and sugar. Spread evenly over cheesecake. Return to oven and bake an additional 5 minutes. Refrigerate. Serve chilled.

This is one of Mom's signature pies. She had made this pie long before I was born. We all loved it and so did our friends and catering customers. Mom always drizzled something yummy on top like a raspberry sauce or a blackberry sauce made with our wild blackberries.

185

Oregon Apple Dapple

Serves: 8

¼ **cup butter, softened**
1 **cup sugar**
1 **egg**
1 **cup all-purpose flour**
1 **teaspoon baking soda**
¼ **teaspoon salt**
1 **teaspoon cinnamon**
¼ **teaspoon ground nutmeg**
1 **teaspoon vanilla**
2 **cups grated apples**
¼ **cup chopped nuts (optional)**

Preheat oven to 350 degrees. Cream butter and sugar in a large bowl. Beat in egg. In a separate bowl, combine flour, baking soda, salt, cinnamon, and nutmeg. Stir into creamed mixture. Add vanilla, apples, and nuts. Pour batter evenly into a greased 8x8x2-inch baking dish. Bake for 35-40 minutes. Serve warm.

We enjoyed testing this very moist cake. My tasters decided it would be great served with whipped cream or vanilla ice cream. It is an old recipe of Mom's that she served long ago.

Wild Rice Pudding with Pears

Serves: 8

Pudding

¹/₂	**cup uncooked wild rice**
1 ¹/₄	**cups milk**
4	**egg yolks**
²/₃	**cup sugar**
³/₄	**cup milk, heated**
1	**teaspoon vanilla**
1 ¹/₂	**envelopes unflavored gelatin**
3	**tablespoons warm water**

Pears and Sauce

4	**Bartlett pears, cored and sliced in half**
2	**cups white Zinfandel wine**
2	**sticks cinnamon**
¹/₂	**cup sugar**
1	**teaspoon lemon rind**
	Whipped cream, sweetened

Wash rice and cover with water by 2 inches. Bring to boil, uncovered. Reduce heat and simmer 45 minutes. Rinse rice under running water and return to pan. Add milk. Cook about 20 minutes or until tender. Set aside. Combine egg yolks and sugar in the top of a double boiler. Do not allow the water to splash into the small pan. Stir in hot milk. Add vanilla and cook over boiling water until thickened, stirring constantly. Mix gelatin and warm water in a small cup until gelatin dissolves. Stir gelatin into egg yolk mixture. Remove from heat. Pour mixture into a medium bowl and cool. Add rice to egg mixture and mix well. Pour rice mixture into a 4-cup mold and refrigerate. For the sauce, combine pears, white Zinfandel, cinnamon sticks, sugar, and lemon rind in a saucepan. Simmer, uncovered, about 15 minutes. Strain pears from sauce and place in a bowl. Cook sauce for 15 minutes until reduced. Cool slightly. Invert rice pudding onto a platter. Arrange pears around sides of rice pudding. Pour sauce over all. Decorate with whipped cream.

Sherry Wine Cake with Brandy Topping   Serves: 10

Cake

1   **package (18 ounces) yellow cake mix**

1   **package (3 ounces) French vanilla instant pudding mix**

4   **eggs**

¾   **cup sherry**

¾   **cup canola oil**

1   **teaspoon ground nutmeg**

Brandy Topping

1   **cup heavy cream**

¼   **cup powdered sugar**

2   **tablespoons apricot brandy or other fruit flavored brandy**

Preheat oven to 350 degrees. Beat cake mix, pudding mix, eggs, sherry, oil, and nutmeg in a bowl until creamy. Pour batter into a greased Bundt pan. Bake for 45 minutes. Cool cake to room temperature. For the topping, whip together cream and powdered sugar until stiff peaks form. Add brandy and mix well. Serve a heaping tablespoon of topping on each cake slice.

Thanks to our friends, Nancy and Marty Smith, this cake now comes with a brandy topping. The cake is flavorful and very moist. I thought it would taste great with some Grand Marnier drizzled over the top. Nancy and Marty went a step further and came up with the brandy topping. I love it! The cake would also be wonderful with fresh sliced fruit.

188

DESSERTS

Pumpkin Pecan Spice Cake

Serves: 12

Cake

1   package (18 ounces) carrot cake mix or spice cake mix

½   can (15 ounces) pumpkin

½   cup canola oil

1   package (3 ounces) instant vanilla pudding mix

3   eggs

1   teaspoon cinnamon

½   cup water

½   cup chopped pecans

Frosting

1   package (16 ounces) powdered sugar

½   cup butter, softened

¼   teaspoon salt

½   teaspoon vanilla

½   cup milk

Preheat oven to 350 degrees. Beat cake mix, pumpkin, oil, pudding mix, eggs, cinnamon, water, and pecans in a bowl. Pour batter into a 13x9x2-inch baking dish. Bake for 40 minutes. Cool completely. For the frosting, blend powdered sugar, butter, salt, vanilla, and milk until creamy. Frost cooled cake. Let cake set about 1 hour. Cut into squares.

Mom originally had the spice cake mix on the recipe. I decided to substitute a carrot cake mix because I had such a difficult time finding the spice cake mix in our area. I thought if I had a hard time, others might too. The carrot cake mix ended up being a great substitute. Everyone loved it when I served it on Easter. The cake is flavorful and very moist, and the frosting does not overpower the cake.

189

Cherry Angel Cake

Serves: 10

Cake

1	large store bought angel food cake, (larger than 7 ounces)

Frosting

1	cup powdered sugar
18	ounces cream cheese, softened
1	envelope (1.3 ounces) dream whip

Glaze

1	can (21 ounces) cherry pie filling
1/4	teaspoon cinnamon
1/2	teaspoon salt

Slice cake in half horizontally through the center. In a small mixing bowl, beat powdered sugar and cream cheese until creamy. Beat in dream whip. In a separate bowl, combine pie filling, cinnamon, and salt. Spread half frosting over bottom cake layer. Spoon one-third glaze over frosting. The glaze will run down the sides. Place top cake layer over glaze. Frost top layer with remaining frosting. Drizzle remaining glaze over top. Refrigerate at least 4 hours before serving. Serve chilled.

The frosting makes this angel food cake into a very rich dessert. It looks pretty with the cherry filling drizzled over the top. I suggest making the angel food cake per the instructions on a 16 ounce box of Angel Food Cake Mix or buying a large angel food cake. Many of the cakes I have seen in bakeries are too small.

DESSERTS

Texas Cake

Serves: 10

Cake

2 cups sugar
2 cups all-purpose flour
2 teaspoons cinnamon
1/2 teaspoon salt
1/2 cup butter
1/4 cup cocoa powder
1/2 cup vegetable shortening
1 cup water
2 eggs, beaten
1 teaspoon vanilla
1/2 cup buttermilk
1 teaspoon baking soda

Frosting

1/2 cup butter
4 squares (1 ounce each) semi-sweet chocolate
6 tablespoons milk
1 package (16 ounces) powdered sugar
1 cup chopped pecans

Preheat oven to 400 degrees. Combine sugar, flour, cinnamon, and salt in a large bowl. In a saucepan, combine butter, cocoa, shortening, and water. Bring to boil. Reduce heat and cook until smooth and creamy. Add to flour mixture and mix well. In a separate bowl, blend eggs, vanilla, buttermilk, and baking soda. Add to flour mixture and stir by hand until well combined. Pour batter into a 13x9x2-inch baking dish. Bake 20 minutes or until cake springs back when touched in the middle. Do not overcook as this cake is meant to be very moist. Make frosting while the cake is cooling slightly. Cook and stir butter and chocolate in a small saucepan until smooth. Stir in milk. Add powdered sugar and pecans and mix well. Spread the frosting immediately over hot cake. Cool and cut into squares.

Mom and Dad's friends, Maggie and Rich Hearney, shared this recipe a few years ago. It is a very moist cake, almost like a brownie. The cinnamon adds to the rich chocolate flavor of this cake.

191

Norma's Almond Cake   Serves: 15

Cake

1	cup butter or margarine
1	cup water
2	cups sifted all-purpose flour
2	cups sugar
2	eggs, beaten
1/2	cup sour cream
2	teaspoons almond extract
1	teaspoon salt
1	teaspoon baking soda

Frosting

1/2	cup butter or margarine
1/4	cup milk
4 1/2	cups powdered sugar
1/2	teaspoon almond extract

Preheat oven to 375 degrees. In large saucepan, bring butter and water to boil. Remove from heat. Stir in flour, sugar, eggs, sour cream, almond extract, salt, and baking soda until smooth. Pour batter into a greased 15x10x1-inch baking dish. Bake 20-22 minutes or until cake is golden browned and a toothpick comes out clean when inserted in the middle. Cool 20 minutes. For the frosting, combine butter and milk in a saucepan. Bring to boil. Remove from heat. Gradually add powdered sugar and almond extract. Mix well. Spread over warm cake. Cut into squares and serve at room temperature.

Our close friend, Norma Dunsing, gave this recipe to Mom several years ago. This recipe and The Brownie Cake recipe became Jeanette's Country Cooking's most served desserts next to her homemade fruit pies. She would make several huge restaurant pans at a time and freeze them a week before the catering job. She liked to serve it sometimes with a drizzle of raspberry sauce or jam.

The Brownie Cake

Serves: 15

Brownie

2 cups all-purpose flour, sifted

2 cups sugar

1 cup butter

4 tablespoons cocoa powder

1 cup water

¼ cup sour milk or 1 tablespoon vinegar added to ¼ cup milk

1 teaspoon vanilla

1 teaspoon baking soda

2 eggs, beaten

Frosting

¼ cup butter

2 tablespoons cocoa powder

3 tablespoons milk

2¼ cups powdered sugar

1 teaspoon vanilla

Preheat oven to 350 degrees. In a large bowl, combine flour and sugar. Set aside. In a large saucepan, bring butter, cocoa, and water to boil. Remove from heat and pour over flour mixture. Whisk batter until smooth. Stir in sour milk, vanilla, and baking soda. Add eggs and stir until well blended. Pour batter into a greased 15x10x1-inch baking dish. Bake 8-10 minutes or until a toothpick comes out clean when inserted in the middle. Cool 5 minutes. For the frosting, melt butter in a saucepan. Remove from heat. Add cocoa, milk, powdered sugar, and vanilla and mix well. Spread frosting over warm cake.

Correction: Bake 18-20 minutes . . .

This is the famous recipe that was probably served to most everyone in Mendocino County! It came from our friend, Gracia Slater, who worked for Mom for 9½ years. Gracia is an amazing baker. I fondly remember her making this cake and Mom's sugar cookies. Lots of them!

COUNTRY COOKING

Carrot Cake

Serves: 12

Cake

2   cups all-purpose flour
2   cups sugar
2   teaspoons cinnamon
2   teaspoons baking soda
1   teaspoon salt
4   eggs, beaten
1½ cups vegetable oil
3   cups shredded carrots

Cream Cheese Frosting

½   cup butter, softened
1   package (8 ounces) cream cheese, softened
4   cups powdered sugar
1   teaspoon vanilla

Preheat oven to 350 degrees. Combine flour, sugar, cinnamon, baking soda, and salt. Add eggs, oil, and carrots. Mix well. Pour batter into a greased 13x9x2-inch baking dish. Bake 40-45 minutes or until firm. Cream butter and cream cheese until smooth. Beat in powdered sugar and vanilla. Spread frosting over cooled cake.

This is an incredible recipe that can easily be tripled into large restaurant style pans. Mom used this recipe all year long for her clients. Mom's friend, Gary Venturi, shared this one with Mom when the catering business first started. Gary worked for Mom prepping food in the kitchen. He brought this recipe to the kitchen one day and it became one of our most popular recipes.

194

Spice Cake

Serves: 12

2	**cups water**
2	**cups raisins**
1	**cup vegetable shortening**
2	**cups sugar**
3	**cups all-purpose flour**
2	**teaspoons baking soda**
½	**teaspoon salt**
1	**teaspoon cinnamon**
½	**teaspoon ground allspice**
½	**teaspoon ground nutmeg**
½	**teaspoon ground cloves**

Preheat oven to 350 degrees. Combine water, raisins, shortening, and sugar in a saucepan. Bring to boil. Cook and stir until sugar melts. Let cool. Combine flour, baking soda, and salt. Beat into raisin mixture. Add cinnamon, allspice, nutmeg, and cloves. Mix well. Pour batter into a greased 10-inch tube pan. Bake for 1 hour.

I do not remember Mom using this in the catering business, but on the recipe is a note that says, "Delicious." I included all recipes that she wrote that on because I knew they would be great. You will love the moist texture and spicy flavor of this cake. The raisins are a must!

195

Apple Cake

Serves: 12

1   cup vegetable oil
2   cups sugar
3   eggs, beaten
1   teaspoon vanilla
2   cups all-purpose flour
1   teaspoon baking powder
½   teaspoon salt
1   teaspoon cinnamon
4   cups peeled and diced apples
1   cup chopped walnuts (optional)
3   tablespoons powdered sugar

Preheat oven to 350 degrees. Cream oil and sugar in a large bowl. Stir in eggs and vanilla. Mix well. Add flour, baking powder, salt, cinnamon, apples, and walnuts. Pour batter into a 13x9x2-inch baking dish. Bake 45 minutes or until firm. Sprinkle with powdered sugar. Serve either warm or room temperature.

This recipe came from my Grandma Stroh. She was an amazing cook and was an inspiration to Mom. My dad loved this recipe all over again when I tested it on him. It is very dense and wonderfully moist.

196

DESSERTS

Dried Fruit Medley Cake with Late Harvest Zinfandel

Serves: 10

1	cup dried peaches, chopped
1	cup dried pears, chopped
1	cup dried nectarines, chopped
1	cup vegetable oil
4	eggs
2	cups sugar
½	cup buttermilk
½	cup late-harvest Zinfandel wine
2	cups all-purpose flour
1	teaspoon cinnamon
1	teaspoon ground nutmeg
1	teaspoon apple pie seasoning
1	teaspoon ground cloves
1	teaspoon salt
1	teaspoon baking soda
1	teaspoon baking powder

Preheat oven to 325 degrees. Beat peaches, pears, nectarines, oil, eggs, sugar, buttermilk, and Zinfandel until well blended. In a separate bowl, combine flour, cinnamon, nutmeg, apple pie seasoning, cloves, salt, baking soda, and baking powder. Add dry ingredients to dried fruit mixture. Beat until smooth. Pour mixture into a greased tube pan or a 9-inch springform pan. Bake for 1 hour, 30 minutes.

This is a very moist cake. Looking at the notes on this recipe, it came from Pat Denny and Mom when they first started Jeanette's Country Cooking together in 1986. This recipe was also featured in the article about Mom in the January 1993 issue of Country America *magazine.*

197

Black Bottom Cupcakes

Yields: 16 cupcakes

Cupcakes

1½ cups all-purpose flour
1 cup sugar
¼ cup cocoa powder
1 teaspoon baking soda
½ teaspoon salt
1 cup water
5 tablespoons vegetable oil
1 tablespoon cider vinegar
1 teaspoon vanilla

Cream Cheese Topping

1 package (8 ounces) cream cheese, softened
1 egg
⅓ cup sugar
1 package (6 ounces) milk chocolate chips
½ cup finely chopped walnuts

Preheat oven to 350 degrees. In a large bowl, combine flour, sugar, cocoa, baking soda, and salt. In another bowl, blend water, oil, vinegar, and vanilla until creamy. Gradually add to dry ingredients and mix well. Spoon batter into 16 paper lined cupcake cups filling one-half full. Beat together cream cheese, egg, and sugar. Stir in chocolate chips. Top each cupcake with 1 tablespoon of cream cheese topping. Sprinkle each cupcake evenly with walnuts. Bake 25-30 minutes or until lightly browned.

This heavenly dessert came from our good friend, Gary Venturi, who served it at La Chaumiere Bed and Breakfast in Calistoga. We are so happy he shared this one with us. It received a "10" from our friends, the Smiths! In fact Marty wanted it for his dessert on his birthday.

DESSERTS

Chocolate Cherry Cake

Serves: 10

Cake

1   package (18 ounces) chocolate fudge cake mix
1   can (21 ounces) cherry pie filling
1   teaspoon almond extract
2   eggs, beaten

Frosting

1   cup sugar
5   tablespoons butter
1/3   cup milk
1   cup semi-sweet chocolate chips

Preheat oven to 350 degrees. Grease and flour a 13x9x2-inch baking dish. In a large bowl, combine by hand cake mix, pie filling, almond extract, and eggs. Pour batter into dish. Bake 25 minutes or until a toothpick comes out clean. Let the cake partially cool before frosting it. For the frosting, combine sugar, butter, and milk in a small saucepan. Bring to boil. Boil for 1 minute, stirring constantly. Remove from heat. Stir in chocolate chips until smooth. Pour frosting over cake and let cool.

This is my Grandma Stroh's recipe. It is so moist and delicious!

199

Jeanette's Pie Dough

Yields: 1 double pie crust

2½ cups pastry flour

1 teaspoon salt

1 cup vegetable shortening, room temperature

½ cup water, room temperature

Mix flour and salt in a small bowl. Cut in shortening with a pastry blender until crumbly. Add water and mix with a fork into a loose ball of dough. It is very important to handle the dough as little as possible and not work hard to make it into a firm piece of dough.

Single crust preparation:
Pour the loose dough onto a large floured surface. Work the dough with your hands until it is combined enough to split into two balls. Roll first ball with a rolling pin into an 11-inch round. Fold the round in half and place on one side of a 9½-inch pie plate. Unfold dough to cover the pie plate and sides evenly. Lightly press dough into the bottom and sides of the pie plate. Using floured fingers, pinch the dough or make a scalloped decoration around the pie plate. Make sure dough is securely attached to the rim of the pie plate so crust does not slide down the sides during baking. Depending on your recipe, it may ask you to have a baked or unbaked shell. For a baked shell, bake at 350 degrees for 30 minutes. For an unbaked shell, pour filling into the crust and bake as instructed in the recipe. Wrap the second ball with plastic wrap and keep in the refrigerator.

DESSERTS

Double crust preparation:

Pour the loose dough onto a large floured surface. Work the dough with your hands until it is combined enough to split into two balls. Roll first ball with a rolling pin into an 11-inch round. Fold the round in half and place on one side on a 9½-inch pie plate. Unfold dough to cover the pie plate and sides evenly. Lightly press dough into the bottom and sides of plate. Fill with your favorite filling. Roll second ball into an 11-inch round. Fold in half and place over the top of your filling. Unfold the dough to cover the bottom dough evenly around the pie plate.

Using floured fingers, fold top dough under the bottom dough all the way around the pie plate. Make sure the dough is evenly distributed around the rim of the pie plate. Using your fingers, pinch the dough or make a scalloped decoration around the pie plate. Do not pinch the dough too high or it will fall over as it bakes. Keep the dough close to the rim of the pie tin. Bake pie as instructed in the recipe.

Mom began Jeanette's Country Cooking with her famous pies. She made them in the kitchen of the house we grew up in and sold them to our local store in Potter Valley. Later when the catering kitchen was built, she would make up to 88 pies for Thanksgiving to sell to individuals. She was amazing to watch. Thankfully, I watched her all those years so I could share with you her pie dough recipe. Enjoy!

201

Mud Pie

Serves: 12

Crust

**20 chocolate sandwich cookies
with crème filling, crushed**

¼ cup butter, melted

Filling

**1 container (1¾ quart) coffee
ice cream, softened**

Frosting

¼ cup butter, melted

**1 can (5 ounces) evaporated
milk**

¾ cup sugar

**1 package (6 ounces) milk
chocolate chips**

½ cup chopped walnuts

In a small bowl, combine cookie crumbs and butter. Press mixture evenly onto the bottom of a 13x9x2-inch baking dish. Spread ice cream evenly over crust. Freeze until ice cream has hardened. For the frosting, combine butter, evaporated milk, and sugar in a small saucepan. Cook and stir over low heat until sugar dissolves. Add chocolate chips and continue stirring over low heat until chocolate melts and mixture is a smooth consistency. Set aside and cool. Spread cooled chocolate mixture evenly over ice cream. Sprinkle with nuts. Return to freezer until ready to serve. Cut into 12 squares.

I am so thankful to our close friend, Dolores Hamilton, for sharing this incredible recipe with me in honor of Mom. Dolores worked for Mom as one of our event staff during the final years of Jeanette's Country Cooking. All of our tasters loved this recipe and would have had seconds if they weren't so full! It is very rich.

DESSERTS

Apple Pie

Serves: 8

7 medium Granny Smith apples, cored, peeled and sliced

1½ cups sugar

1 teaspoon cinnamon

¼ cup all-purpose flour

Jeanette's Pie Dough recipe (see page 200)

Preheat oven to 350 degrees. In a large bowl, combine apples, sugar, cinnamon, and flour. The sugar mixture should be evenly distributed over the apples. Press pie dough into a 9½-inch pie plate. Spoon apple mixture over dough. Cover with second half of rolled-out dough. Pinch dough together to seal edges. With a fork, pierce an "A" into the top to allow steam to escape. Place pie on a baking sheet. Place the baking sheet on the rack just below the middle. Bake for 1 hour, 15 minutes. You will know the pie is finished when any drips that come out are very thick and the crust is slightly golden browned.

This is Mom's signature pie. It would have been interesting to figure out how many apple pies she made in her lifetime. Mom always used Granny Smith apples; other apples are too watery for the pie.

203

Wild Blackberry Pie

Serves: 8

4   cups wild blackberries
1½ cups sugar
¼   cup all-purpose flour
Jeanette's Pie Dough recipe
(see page 200)

Preheat oven to 350 degrees. Combine blackberries, sugar, and flour in a bowl. Press pie dough into a 9½-inch pie plate. Pour filling over dough. Cover with second half of rolled-out dough. Pinch dough together to seal edges. Place the pie on a baking sheet. Place the baking sheet on the rack just below the middle. Bake for 1 hour, 15 minutes. You will know the pie is finished when any drips that come out are very thick and the crust is slightly golden browned.

Potter Valley is noted for its wild blackberries. They are small and flavorful. The fences on our ranch are lined with these delicious berries. We picked the berries and froze them in 4-cup freezer bags to be used all year long. Mom would make sure we froze enough berries to make at least 300 pies a year.

204

DESSERTS

Lemon Meringue Pie   Serves: 8

Filling

1½ cups sugar
⅓ cup cornstarch
1½ cups water
3 egg yolks
3 tablespoons butter
½ cup lemon juice
1 single pie crust, baked (see *Jeanette's Pie Dough recipe, page 200)*

Meringue

3 egg whites
6 tablespoons sugar

Preheat oven to 350 degrees. Be sure to save the egg whites! In a saucepan, whisk together sugar, cornstarch, water, and egg yolks. Bring to boil. Boil 1 minute. The mixture will be very thick. Remove from heat. Add butter and lemon juice. Stir until smooth. Pour filling into baked pie crust. Beat egg whites and sugar until stiff peaks form. Spread meringue evenly over filling. Make decorative peaks on meringue. Place on the bottom rack of the oven. Bake 20 minutes or until peaks are golden browned.

It was such a treat when Mom would make a lemon meringue pie. I was so happy to stir the pot while it came to a boil because I was assured I could "lick the pan" after it was ready. Mom always used Meyer lemons from Grandma Nancy's tree that grew beautifully in Burlingame, CA. We would pick the lemons, juice them and freeze the juice for future pies.

Peanut Butter Pie

Serves: 12

Crust

1   **package (9 ounces) thin chocolate wafer cookies, crushed**
4   **tablespoons butter, melted**

Filling

1   **cup peanut butter, creamy or chunky**
1   **package (8 ounces) cream cheese, softened**
1   **cup sugar**
2   **tablespoons butter, melted**
1   **cup frozen whipped topping, thawed**
1   **teaspoon vanilla**

Topping

4   **squares (1 ounce each) semi-sweet chocolate**
½   **cup sour cream**

Combine cookie crumbs and butter. Press mixture onto the bottom and up the sides of a 9-inch pie plate. Cream peanut butter, cream cheese, sugar, and butter. Fold in whipped topping and vanilla. Pour peanut butter mixture into the crust. Freeze. For the topping, melt the chocolate in top of a double boiler. Remove from heat. Stir in sour cream. Spread topping over filling. Refrigerate for a few hours. Serve chilled.

The tasters loved this one — especially my peanut butter lovers. It is very rich and flavorful. Small pieces will be plenty for your guests!

206

DESSERTS

Chocolate Cream Pie   Serves: 8

¹⁄₃ **cup milk**

¹⁄₂ **cup powdered sugar**

1   **teaspoon vanilla**

1   **package (8 ounces) cream cheese, softened**

1   **package (6 ounces) instant chocolate pudding mix**

2¹⁄₃ **cups milk**

1   **single pie crust, baked and cooled *(see Jeanette's Pie Dough recipe, page 200)***

1   **container (8 ounces) frozen whipped topping, thawed**

Blend milk, powdered sugar, vanilla, and cream cheese in a food processor. Add pudding mix and remaining milk and mix thoroughly. Pour filling into baked crust. Spread topping over filling. Refrigerate until ready to serve. Serve chilled.

This is one of those recipes Mom created that everyone loved. She would get huge orders for these pies, even at Thanksgiving! It is best to make it the day of your dinner party so the bottom of the pie does not get too wet from the pudding.

207

COUNTRY COOKING

Pecan Pie   Serves: 8

¼ cup butter, softened
1   cup sugar
3   eggs, well beaten
1   cup dark corn syrup
1   teaspoon vanilla
½ teaspoon salt
1   cup pecan halves
1   single pie crust, unbaked
    *(see Jeanette's Pie Dough
    recipe, page 200)*

Preheat oven to 350 degrees. Cream butter and sugar. Beat in eggs. Add corn syrup, vanilla, and salt. Mix well. Spread pecans evenly on bottom of pie crust. Pour filling over pecans. Bake for 1 hour.

This is my sister's favorite pie. Every Thanksgiving Mom made sure Kathy had her pecan pie! When I tested the recipe, she was very happy to be the taster. It passed with flying colors!

208

Strawberry Gelatin Pie

Serves: 8

1 **package (3 ounces) strawberry flavored gelatin**

½ **cup boiling water**

½ **cup sugar**

½ **cup cold water**

1 **package (12 ounces) cold strawberries, washed, stemmed and sliced**

1 **single pie crust, baked and cooled *(see Jeanette's Pie Dough recipe, page 200)***

1 **container (8 ounces) frozen whipped topping, thawed**

Dissolve gelatin in boiling water. Stir in sugar until dissolved. Add cold water and mix well. Set aside and cool at room temperature for 30 minutes. Arrange strawberries evenly on the bottom of baked pie crust. Pour gelatin mixture evenly over strawberries. Let cool and refrigerate. Top with whipped topping just before serving.

This is our favorite summer pie. Mom would sometimes add a ripe mashed banana or a small can of crushed pineapple to the bottom of the pie with a smaller amount of strawberries and pour the gelatin mixture over the fruit.

209

Grandma Nancy's Peanut Butter Cookies

Yields: 4 dozen cookies

1   cup chunky peanut butter
½   cup vegetable shortening
1   package (18 ounces) yellow cake mix
2   eggs
2   tablespoons water
1   teaspoon vanilla
Sugar

Preheat oven to 350 degrees. In a large mixing bowl, cut peanut butter and shortening into cake mix using an electric mixer on low speed. Add eggs, water, and vanilla. Mix well to form the dough. Shape dough into 1 ½-inch balls. Place balls on a baking sheet and flatten each with a fork dipped in sugar. Bake for 10 minutes.

Grandma Nancy McRoberts called this an all-American cookie recipe. She enjoyed baking and was an inspiration to my mom. I thought it was appropriate to have a peanut butter recipe in the book to honor Mom's first try at cooking when she placed her brother's prized butterfly collection into a jar of peanut butter and said she was making it better. I love that story and found that Mom continued changing recipes through the years to make them taste better.

DESSERTS

Oatmeal Molasses Cookies

Yields: 3½ dozen cookies

1¾ cups all-purpose flour
1 teaspoon baking soda
1 teaspoon baking powder
½ teaspoon salt
2 eggs
1¼ cups sugar
1 teaspoon cinnamon
2 cups old-fashioned rolled oats
6 tablespoons molasses
1 cup raisins

Preheat oven to 350 degrees. In a large bowl, combine flour, baking soda, baking powder, and salt. In a separate bowl, combine eggs, sugar, cinnamon, oats, molasses, and raisins. Add oat mixture to dry mixture and mix well. Roll dough into 1-inch balls and place on a baking sheet. Bake for 12 minutes.

Mom wrote "good" on this recipe so I knew I wanted to print it in the cookbook. They are chewy and have a rich molasses flavor. They were a big hit with my daughter, Amanda, and our tasters.

211

Refrigerator Cookies

Yields: 4 dozen cookies

1	cup vegetable shortening
1/2	cup sugar
1/2	cup packed brown sugar
2	eggs
2 3/4	cups all-purpose flour
1/2	teaspoon baking soda
1	teaspoon salt
3	teaspoons cinnamon

Cream shortening, sugar, brown sugar, and eggs. Add flour, baking soda, salt, and cinnamon. Mix well. Press dough into two balls and squeeze them several times to make sure all ingredients are well combined. Roll each ball into a 14-inch long log on a lightly floured board. Wrap each log in wax paper and refrigerate overnight. Slice each log into 24 round slices. Bake at 400 degrees for 6-8 minutes.

Mom had this recipe written on an old recipe card from my childhood days. I don't remember the recipe, but after testing it I consider it now my favorite cinnamon cookie. I have always liked a good snickerdoodle recipe, but this one beats them all. I enjoy them with a cup of hot chamomile tea or a big glass of cold milk.

DESSERTS

Salted Peanut Cookies

Yields: 4 dozen cookies

1 **cup vegetable shortening**
1 **cup packed brown sugar**
1 **cup sugar**
2 **eggs**
1 **teaspoon vanilla**
2 **cups all-purpose flour**
½ **teaspoon baking soda**
1 **teaspoon baking powder**
1 **cup salted peanuts**
1 **cup coarsely crushed corn flakes**
1 **cup old-fashioned rolled oats**
Sugar

Cream shortening, brown sugar, sugar, eggs, and vanilla. Add flour, baking soda, baking powder, peanuts, corn flakes, and oats. Mix well. Refrigerate 1 hour. Roll dough into 1 ½-inch balls. Roll in sugar. Place on a baking sheet 2-inches apart. Bake at 375 degrees for 10 minutes.

What an amazing cookie! They are very unique with a big crunch of peanuts and corn flakes. All of the tasters loved this one.

213

Scotch Shortbread

Yields: 32 wedges

1 **cup butter, softened**
½ **cup sugar**
2½ **cups all-purpose flour**

Preheat oven to 300 degrees. Beat butter until creamy. Gradually add sugar and mix well. Gradually add flour and mix well. Roll dough into a circle about ¼-inch thick. Cut dough into pie-shaped wedges. Place on a greased baking sheet. Pierce the wedges with a fork before baking. Bake 30 minutes or until lightly browned.

Mom loved shortbread, and so do I! Mom had Scotch in her, so I thought it was only appropriate to place this recipe in the cookbook.

DESSERTS

Oklahoma Sugar Cookies

Yields: 5 dozen cookies

1   **cup butter, softened**

2   **cups sugar**

2   **eggs**

1   **cup vegetable oil**

1   **teaspoon vanilla**

5   **cups all-purpose flour**

2   **teaspoons baking soda**

½   **teaspoon salt**

2   **teaspoons baking powder**

¼   **cup sugar**

Preheat oven to 350 degrees. Cream butter, sugar, eggs, oil, and vanilla in a large bowl. In a smaller bowl, mix flour, baking soda, salt, and baking powder. Add to creamed mixture and mix well. Roll dough into 1-inch balls and place on a baking sheet. Pour sugar into a bowl. Dip a fork into the sugar and then crisscross each cookie with the sugared fork. Bake for 10 minutes.

Mom and I talked about keeping this recipe out of the cookbook just in case we wanted to market it through PJ's Gourmet. It is that good! I decided I wanted to stick with bottled specialty foods and placed it in Mom's cookbook for you. This is an old recipe from our Oklahoma relatives. Annie Laurie from Elgin, Oklahoma made these cookies for us at a family reunion over 30 years ago. Mom sold these cookies to local stores when she first started catering. She kept this recipe very close to her. Only a few people have it. Now it's yours! Try just the dough. It is one of my favorites next to chocolate chip cookie dough.

215

Pecan Cookies

Yields: 6 dozen cookies

1   **cup butter**
1   **cup sugar**
1   **cup packed brown sugar**
1   **egg**
1   **cup canola oil**
1   **cup old-fashioned rolled oats**
1   **cup crushed crisp rice cereal**
½   **cup chopped pecans**
3½   **cups sifted all-purpose flour**
1   **teaspoon baking soda**
1   **teaspoon salt**
2   **teaspoons almond extract**

Preheat oven to 325 degrees. Cream butter, sugar, and brown sugar until light and fluffy. Add egg and mix well. Stir in oil, mixing well. Add oats, cereal, pecans, flour, baking soda, salt, and almond extract. Mix thoroughly. Shape dough into small balls. Place on a baking sheet. Flatten with a fork. Bake for 12 minutes. Cool a few minutes before removing from baking sheet.

This is a secret recipe we decided to publish. These cookies were made into large 6-inch cookies and sold at our local stores. Everyone loved these crunchy, almond flavored cookies!

DESSERTS

Chocolate Chip Cookies

Yields: 3½ dozen cookies

1 cup vegetable shortening
¾ cup sugar
1 cup packed brown sugar
1 teaspoon vanilla
2 eggs
2¼ cups all-purpose flour
1 teaspoon baking soda
1 teaspoon salt
1 package (12 ounces) milk chocolate chips

Preheat oven to 350 degrees. Cream shortening, sugar, brown sugar, and vanilla in a large bowl. Add eggs and mix well. Stir in flour, baking soda, and salt. Mix well. Stir in chocolate chips. Drop dough by rounded tablespoonfuls onto a baking sheet. Bake 10 minutes or until golden browned.

These are great cookies. We always use milk chocolate chips and not the semi-sweet because they just taste better. Why bake with semi-sweet when you can use milk chocolate to make it sweeter?

217

Cinnamon Crispies

Serves: 6

Pie dough for single crust
(see Jeanette's Pie Dough
recipe, page 200)
¼ **cup butter, melted**
3 **teaspoons cinnamon**
½ **cup sugar**

Preheat oven to 350 degrees. Roll out pie pastry on a floured board into a 10x12-inch rectangle. Place pastry on a baking pan. Spread butter evenly over pastry. Sprinkle cinnamon evenly over butter. Top with sugar. Bake 30 minutes or until sides are golden browned. Cut into squares. Serve at room temperature.

This is a fun recipe to do when you have made a pie dough recipe and only needed a single crust. The other half of the dough will not go to waste when you use this yummy recipe! These were a big hit for my Dad, sister, and me. We looked forward to Mom making a lemon meringue or a pecan pie because we knew she had to do something with the other half of the dough.

DESSERTS

Sesame Seed Cookies

Yields: 4 dozen cookies

2   cups butter, softened
1½ cups sugar
2   cups shredded coconut
3   cups all-purpose flour
½   cup finely chopped walnuts
1   cup sesame seeds

Preheat oven to 300 degrees. Cream butter and sugar. Add coconut, flour, walnuts, and sesame seeds. Divide dough in half. Roll each half into a 12-inch long log. Wrap each log with plastic wrap. Refrigerate until firm. Slice each log into 24 small slices. Place flat on a baking sheet 2-inches apart. Bake 20-30 minutes or until golden browned around the bottom edges.

Pat Denny shared this recipe with Mom. I love the sesame and coconut flavor of these small cookies. They are so unique!

219

Russian Teacakes

Yields: 4 dozen cookies

1 **cup butter, softened**
½ **cup powdered sugar**
1 **teaspoon vanilla**
2¼ **cups all-purpose flour**
¼ **teaspoon salt**
¾ **cup walnuts, finely chopped**
Powdered sugar

Preheat oven to 350 degrees. Cream butter, powdered sugar, and vanilla. Sift together flour and salt. Add to creamed mixture. Mix in nuts. Roll dough into 1-inch balls. Place on a baking sheet. Bake for 10-12 minutes. While still warm, roll the balls in powdered sugar. Cool and roll in powdered sugar.

This was one of Mom's favorite cookie recipes. She would freeze these several days before catering jobs and served them on beautiful glass platters.

DESSERTS

Persimmon Cookies

Yields: 5 dozen cookies

1	cup persimmon pulp
½	teaspoon baking soda
½	teaspoon baking powder
1	cup sugar
½	cup vegetable shortening
1	egg
2	cups all-purpose flour
½	teaspoon cinnamon
½	teaspoon ground cloves
½	teaspoon ground nutmeg
½	teaspoon salt
1	cup walnuts, chopped
1	cup raisins (optional)

Preheat oven to 375 degrees. Beat persimmon pulp in a large bowl. Add baking soda, baking powder, sugar, shortening, and egg and mix well. Add flour, cinnamon, cloves, nutmeg, salt, walnuts, and raisins. Drop dough by teaspoonfuls onto a greased baking sheet. Bake for 12-15 minutes.

We had a persimmon tree on the ranch that produced a little fruit each year. We loved to pick the fruit off the tree and run to the kitchen for Mom to make these yummy cookies. After losing the tree, we searched Potter Valley for trees and found friends who had some. We never went without our annual persimmon cookies! When picking ripe persimmons from a tree or buying at a grocery store, look for ones with a red-orange skin and soft flesh.

221

Rosemary and Pine Nut Squares   Serves: 8

¼ **cup pine nuts**
½ **cup butter**
½ **cup powdered sugar**
1 **tablespoon minced rosemary**
1 **cup all-purpose flour**

Preheat oven to 350 degrees. Spread pine nuts on a baking sheet. Bake until lightly toasted. Set aside. Melt butter in a small saucepan. Stir in powdered sugar, pine nuts, and rosemary. Add flour and mix well. Pour batter into an 8x8x2-inch baking dish. Bake for 20 minutes. Cool and cut into squares.

Our close friend, Norma Dunsing, shared this with Mom. I remember when Mom first tried this recipe. I couldn't imagine rosemary could taste good in a cookie, but I was wrong. This is a unique recipe and one people will continue to talk about.

Chewy Noels

Serves: 8

2	tablespoons butter
1/3	cup all-purpose flour
1/8	teaspoon baking soda
1/8	teaspoon salt
1	cup packed brown sugar
1	cup chopped walnuts
2	eggs, beaten
1	teaspoon vanilla

Powdered sugar, sifted

Preheat oven to 350 degrees. Melt butter in an 8x8x2-inch baking dish. Combine flour, baking soda, and salt. Stir in brown sugar and nuts. Add eggs and vanilla. Carefully pour batter over butter. Bake for 20 minutes. Sprinkle with powdered sugar. Invert cake onto a wire rack and let cool. Sprinkle powdered sugar on top side. Cut into small bars and serve on a platter.

Our close family friend, Norma Dunsing, shared this holiday treat with us. This recipe is a holiday tradition for her family. She writes "Noel" on each bar through the powdered sugar. I decided this recipe would be a favorite of mine all year long!

Lemon Bars   Serves: 10

1   cup butter, softened
½   cup powdered sugar
2   cups all-purpose flour
4   eggs
2   cups sugar
½   cup lemon juice
3   lemons, rind finely grated
¼   cup all-purpose flour
1   tablespoon baking powder
2   tablespoons powdered
    sugar

Preheat oven to 350 degrees. In a bowl, combine butter, sugar, and flour. Spray sides of a 12x7x2-inch baking dish with a non-stick spray. Press mixture onto the bottom of baking dish. Bake for 20 minutes. In a separate bowl, beat together eggs, sugar, lemon juice, lemon rind, flour, and baking powder. Pour filling over baked crust. Bake for 25 minutes. Let cool slightly and cut into squares. While still in the pan, sprinkle with powdered sugar.

Grandma Stroh shared this recipe with Mom. Mom always used the Meyer lemon juice we had frozen from my Grandma Nancy's tree. It is so flavorful compared to the lemon juice you find in stores.

DESSERTS

Sea Foam Candy

Yields: 36 candy pieces

2	egg whites
2	cups sugar
½	cup water
⅛	teaspoon salt
⅛	teaspoon cream of tartar
1	teaspoon vanilla
¼	cup chopped walnuts (optional)

In a medium bowl, beat egg whites until stiff peaks form. Set aside. Combine sugar, water, salt, and cream of tartar in a saucepan. Cover and boil 5 minutes. Uncover and wipe the inside of the saucepan with a damp cloth. Boil without stirring until firm ball stage or a candy thermometer reaches 245 to 248 degrees. Slowly pour sugar mixture over egg whites while beating constantly. Add vanilla and continue beating until stiff peaks form. Stir in walnuts. Quickly drop mixture by teaspoonfuls onto wax paper and cool completely. Remove from wax paper once slightly hardened. Serve at room temperature on a glass platter.

Note: This candy can only be made on a clear day. The candy will not harden on a rainy day.

Our close friend, Kay Whittaker, shared this great, old recipe with us to print in the cookbook in honor of Mom. I remember her making these and divinity when I was a child. It was always a treat to spend time at her house. She said the recipe dates back to 1943 when her good friend, Irene Cherry from Potter Valley, gave it to her.

225

Chocolate Caramel Candy

Yields: 8 dozen candies

Bottom Layer

1 cup milk chocolate chips
¼ cup butterscotch chips
¼ cup creamy peanut butter

Filling

¼ cup butter or margarine
1 cup sugar
¼ cup evaporated milk
1½ cups marshmallow crème
¼ cup creamy peanut butter
1 teaspoon vanilla
1½ cups chopped salted peanuts

Caramel Layer

1 package (14 ounces) caramel candies
¼ cup whipping cream

Icing

1 cup milk chocolate chips
¼ cup butterscotch chips
¼ cup creamy peanut butter

Melt chocolate and butterscotch chips in a small saucepan over low heat until smooth. Add peanut butter and stir until creamy. Spread mixture onto the bottom of a lightly greased 13x9x2-inch baking dish. Refrigerate until set. For filling, melt butter in a heavy saucepan over medium-high heat. Add sugar and milk. Bring to boil. Cook and stir 5 minutes. Remove from heat. Stir in marshmallow crème, peanut butter, and vanilla. Add peanuts. Spread filling over bottom layer. Refrigerate until set. Combine caramels and cream in a saucepan. Stir over low heat until caramel melts and is smooth. Spread caramel mixture over filling. Refrigerate until set. Combine chocolate and butterscotch chips in a small saucepan. Stir over low heat until smooth. Add peanut butter and stir until creamy. Pour over caramel layer. Refrigerate for at least 1 hour. Cut into 1-inch squares. Store in the refrigerator.

DESSERTS

Peanut Butter Bonbons

Yields: 4½ dozen bonbons

½ cup butter, softened

1 package (16 ounces) powdered sugar, sifted

2 cups creamy peanut butter

2 cups crisp rice cereal

1 bar (1.55 ounces) milk chocolate candy

1 package (12 ounces) milk chocolate chips

Paraffin, cut into a 1½x1½-inch square

Combine butter, powdered sugar, and peanut butter in a bowl. Add rice cereal and roll into 1¼-inch balls. Melt candy bar, chocolate chips, and paraffin in the top of a double boiler. Roll balls in chocolate using a spoon. Place balls on wax paper. Serve at room temperature on a glass platter.

This came from our friends, Judy Thornton and Gracia Slater, who worked for Mom for several years. They are both incredible cooks and were such a big part of making Jeanette's Country Cooking a success. We made these bonbons mostly at Christmas time, but they can be enjoyed all year long. My husband ate a dozen in one sitting. He absolutely loves them and so do I.

227

Pat Denny's Truffles

Yields: 50 truffles

7   **tablespoons unsalted butter**
1²/₃ **cups whipping cream**
1   **pound semi-sweet chocolate**
2   **tablespoons Grand Marnier or other liqueur**
Cocoa powder

Heat butter and cream in a saucepan until butter melts. Bring to boil. Remove from heat and add chocolate. Stir until chocolate melts. Cool. Add liqueur and mix well. Cover and refrigerate for 2 hours, stirring every 30 minutes. Refrigerate at least 2 more hours. Sprinkle cocoa powder on a platter. Coat hands with cocoa powder. Roll chocolate into 1-inch balls with hands. Place on a cold platter.

My daughter thought this was the best chocolate recipe ever! Pat Denny, Mom's longtime friend, shared this recipe. It is important to coat your hands with the cocoa powder because the chocolate can be a little sticky. These truffles turn out very soft and are even better the next day.

228

DESSERTS

Tiramisu   Serves: 12

4   eggs yolks
½   cup sugar
2   containers (8 ounces each)
**   mascarpone cheese**
4   egg whites
1   cup espresso or double
**   strength coffee**
½   cup brandy
2   packages (7 ounces each)
**   ladyfingers**
¼   cup cocoa powder
Mint leaves or chocolate curls
**   for garnish**

In a large bowl, beat together egg yolks and sugar with a hand mixer until smooth and creamy. Add mascarpone cheese and continue beating until smooth. In a small bowl, beat egg whites until stiff peaks form. Gently fold egg whites into cheese mixture. Set aside. In another small bowl, blend espresso and brandy. Dip ladyfingers quickly into the espresso mixture, until soaked but not mushy. Arrange a layer of dipped ladyfingers on the bottom of a 13x9x2-inch glass baking dish. Spread half of cheese mixture evenly over ladyfingers. Top with another layer of dipped ladyfingers. Spread remaining cheese mixture over ladyfingers. Dust with cocoa. Refrigerate. Serve chilled. Garnish plates with mint leaves or chocolate curls.

Our close family friends, Martha and Charlie Barra, shared this recipe with Mom several years ago. It is the best tiramisu I have had. All of my tasters loved it! It is very rich and beautiful. The ladyfingers can be found in specialty stores.

229

COUNTRY COOKING

Notes:

INDEX

231

COUNTRY COOKING

INDEX

233

COUNTRY COOKING

234

INDEX

235

INDEX

COUNTRY COOKING

238

INDEX

239

COUNTRY COOKING

NOTES

COUNTRY COOKING

Notes:

NOTES

COUNTRY COOKING

Notes:

in MENDOCINO

Mail to: PJ's Gourmet
PO Box 1
Potter Valley, CA 95469 • www.pjsgourmet.com

Please send _____ copies of

Country Cooking in Mendocino   @ $21.95 each $ _____

Add postage and handling   @ $ 5.00 each $_____

California residents add 7.25% sales tax   @ $ 1.59 each $_____

TOTAL _____

Ship To:
Name _____

Address _____

City _____ State _____ ZIP _____

Please make checks payable to:
PJ's Gourmet

Country Cooking
in MENDOCINO

Mail to: PJ's Gourmet
PO Box 1
Potter Valley, CA 95469 • www.pjsgourmet.com

Please send _____ copies of

Country Cooking in Mendocino   @ $21.95 each $ _____

Add postage and handling   @ $ 5.00 each $_____

California residents add 7.25% sales tax   @ $ 1.59 each $_____

TOTAL _____

Ship To:
Name _____

Address _____

City _____ State _____ ZIP _____

Please make checks payable to:
PJ's Gourmet

ABOUT THE AUTHOR

Debbie Reardan learned the art of country cooking from her mom, Jeanette Stroh. Through Jeanette, Debbie came to understand that a passion for cooking could bridge generations, build relationships, and bring friends together.

Debbie now owns PJ's Gourmet, a specialty food business that sells marinades, sauces, and jams. At home you'll find Debbie in the kitchen making her products, or driving tractors for her dad if she's not horseback riding. Away from the ranch, you'll find her kayaking, hiking, and camping with her family and friends.

Debbie lives on the Stroh Ranch in Potter Valley, California with her husband John, daughter Amanda, and dog Daisy.

247